Self-Publish to a World of Readers

with Amazon, Apple, Google
and other Major Retailers

Jason Matthews

Pismo Beach, California. USA

Subjects include: self-publishing, Kindle, Amazon, Smashwords, Apple iBooks, Barnes & Noble, Google Play, Google Books Partner Center, Kobo, Draft2Digital, CreateSpace, author platform, desktop publishing, formatting ebooks, cover design, marketing, blogging, indie authors, how to publish a book, editing, editors, beta readers, getting reviews and much more.

Also by Jason Matthews

The Little Universe

Jim's Life

Better You, Better Me

Shep Dreams of Home

How to Make, Market and Sell Ebooks All for Free

Get On Google Front Page: SEO Tips for Online Marketing

How to Make Your Own Free Website: And Your Free Blog Too

Table of Contents

Acknowledgments

Many people assisted as this book came together, plus it never would have happened without the thousands of writers and the publishers who've shaped this revolution we're experiencing.

Thank you to the members of my Facebook group for your participation, your feedback and encouragement along the way.

Thank you to all of my beta readers, editors and contributors for catches and suggestions. Thank you especially to Betsi, Angie and Maya; your additions were just what the book needed.

And thank you to the major retailers like Amazon and Smashwords, who were the first to create do-it-yourself platforms for self-publishers. You've empowered us to share stories with readers around the world, indirectly pressuring other retailers to embrace indie authors as well. That's a good thing.

Part 1: A Publishing Dream

Imagine this.

You have a wonderful book inside you.

You spend months to years writing it.

You give it a great title.

An eye-catching cover is designed.

The text is formatted for Kindles, tablets and phones so it looks professional and functions well on any e-reading device.

Your book is published online making it available to readers all over the world.

People sample it and enjoy it.

People buy your book from Amazon, Apple, Google and other retailers.

Amazon, Apple, Google and other retailers send money to your bank account each month.

Your royalties average around 70% of list price, the lion's share of the sale.

Your book receives reviews.

You get emails, interview requests and social media connections from people around the world.

Your network expands.

You decide to write another book.

After imagining this, keep in mind everything above is possible. In fact, it's easily attainable if you've written a great book. The following pages will help inspire everything you've imagined your book can become.

It's Your Book

If you've written a book, you may need to be reminded it's a huge accomplishment. Congratulations on doing that. It can feel like a Herculean task while you're writing. And if you're not quite finished, congrats still because a mostly-finished book represents a ton of effort. In either case, at some point your book will be ready to publish. Then what?

You may have loads of questions.

Who will design the cover and format the interior?

How does one sell from Amazon and major retailers?

Where will I find readers?

How can I market the book without spending a fortune?

You may wonder about ISBN and copyright. You might want an affordable yet competent editor though you have no idea how to find one or what level of editing your book needs. Since the story is part of you, a figurative baby, you're going to do what you can to give it life.

There's a statistic that says 80% of adults have either begun writing a book or want to. Statistics can be unreliable, but this one seems to have merit if you've been following what's happening in the world of publishing. Ebooks and retailers like Amazon changed everything by creating a digital platform where anyone can publish without need of agents or traditional publishing houses. Plus it can be done on any budget. In the grand scheme of things, this has happened in a brief period of time.

An interesting paradox has resulted. Self-publishing is easier than ever, yet harder than ever to do successfully. It's a matter of supply and demand. As the number of new authors releasing books grows exponentially, the number of new readers remains fairly stable. The latter hasn't been able to keep pace and is therefore your primary challenge as an author. These days *it's getting more and more competitive* to get your book in front of readers because of the sheer number of new titles flooding the market.

However it can be done. Many authors make a comfortable living from their books, and you can too. The successful ones may be classified as self-published, independent (indie) or even hybrid authors. Their titles become top sellers on Amazon and the New York Times. In some cases their books generate movie contracts. Their publishing victories often come from doing many things well during the process. Having success with your book may hinge on your response to this recommendation:

Do the little things as well as possible.

That's what this guide focuses on, the myriad of small things that go into your book and its marketing platform. Before publishing through major retail channels like Amazon, Apple, Google, Smashwords and the others we'll get to, you'll discover the little things make a tremendous difference on the bigger picture. They breathe life into all areas of your book.

This guide will lead you into authorship with clearer understanding, better information and a marketing strategy tailored for you. We'll go over what your book needs before publishing to give you methods to handle everything from cover design to interior formatting to marketing. And if your book is already published, you'll learn dozens of things to incorporate into your existing titles to help them sell even better.

You'll have options to fit your skill sets, available time and finances. You can tackle things yourself or hire out wisely. We'll create a strategy for using retailers, like Amazon, and distributors, like Smashwords or BookBaby, to maximize your book's potential to reach any reader no matter where they prefer to purchase. We'll do that and much more.

Get ready to have some fun, learn new things, pull out a few hairs in frustration and sell a lot more books.

True Story

This really happened.

An idea for a book struck me. Call it profound inspiration. In February 2010 I began typing chapter by chapter, writing late into the evenings. Simultaneously I researched my topic because I still had a lot to learn. I designed the book's cover, built a website and blog, then got active with online marketing.

In March, I formatted the interior text and uploaded the book to major retailers. This book was fairly substantial at around 50,000 words. It was also a finished product, not a preorder book set for a future release date. Within hours of publishing, it was listed online for $4.99. The first sales came immediately and I earned 70% of each sale, or $3.49. It was thrilling. All of that happened in 30 days, from original idea to actual sales of the finished product.

How did the book do? Pretty well for a while until it faded in sales. It didn't sell millions of copies but did much better than average for an unknown indie author, selling about 15,000 copies to date. In addition to the money, I've also received emails and made connections with people around the world who read it. Those benefits are the icing on the cake, the networking that begins after people read your book.

This also really happened.

An idea for a book struck me. Call it profound inspiration. I spent 20 years writing it, more off than on. I eventually published it and have sold fewer than 2,000 copies. The money earned barely makes a dent compared to what was spent writing and marketing it, not to mention the thousands of hours working behind the desk.

However, I also consider that book a success. Not financially, but for a writer who had an idea that needed to be expressed. I wrote it as well as I could, and it's out there getting read.

What will your true story be? Time will tell. I hope your experience will include these elements:

- your book will be edited
- the cover will attract attention
- the text will be well-formatted
- readers will enjoy it
- it will be available internationally
- it will have a marketing plan that fits your skill sets, time and finances
- it will lead to meaningful connections

It's tempting to talk about bestsellers, millions of dollars and movie rights, but let's not do that now (even though it's possible). This guide is not about creating hype or false hope; it's about real, practical, easy to follow instructions for getting your book published in the best light possible. Let's focus on doing the little things well to help your dreams become realities. Let's make it happen, whether it takes 30 days or 20 years. Let's get your book out there, ready to be read and enjoyed.

Free PDF Version

There are well over 100 useful hyperlinks within this book. For readers who would appreciate a PDF copy that might be easier to work with the hyperlinks on their computers, just let me know. I offer a free PDF version of this book to any reader who might want one. Further details on how to obtain it are given in the Final Thoughts chapter.

Part 2: Understanding the Basics

Before we get to the nuts and bolts of creating ebooks, let's spend some time walking around describing the scenery. In this section we'll touch on the tasks involved, standards, options and some of the initial decisions you'll need to make. Knowing a bit about Amazon and other retailers will help immensely as you decide on a strategy that suits you best.

Writers also have loads of questions regarding ISBN and copyright. Even though they are unrelated, let's skim the surface on those topics to hopefully answer most questions. Interestingly, some writers worry more about these two things than their marketing plan, but ISBN and copyright are primarily simple tasks.

Step by Step List In No Particular Order

Think about the tasks you'll encounter during the publishing process. Many writers are predicable when it comes to the steps they take to publish a book, doing tasks in order as they approach them. Here's a simplified list of tasks en route to self-publishing.

- write the book
- edit the book
- format the text
- design the cover
- publish the book at online retailers
- market the book

It's common to focus on one task at a time. Writing the book is where most people start. Afterwards they move on to editing, cover design, formatting, etc. until the book has been published. Then the marketing begins. You probably see why this is common, but you may also be thinking of benefits from another method.

Time to think outside the box. In fact, when it comes to anything about the book business, remember to think outside the box. You'll discover this business is full of instances for multiple ways to get things done. Have another look at the same steps, this time in opposite order.

- market the book
- publish the book at online retailers
- design the cover
- format the book
- edit the book
- write the book

With the exception of editing before writing, everything on the list above can actually be done in that order. You can market and publish your book before you've written one chapter. In that case it would be sold as preorders, which we'll discuss, and it represents another example of how fast publishing is changing. Crazy times. I don't recommend doing it exactly in the way above but it is possible. Have a look at the next list.

- design the cover
- market the book
- publish the book at online retailers
- write the book
- format the book
- edit the book

There's no need to think of them as a rigid chronological items. Instead consider these steps as ingredients in a stew, each representing items to add. The stew can still taste delicious even if you don't follow the recipe precisely as it's written. The point of the above lists is to see the wisdom in handling tasks simultaneously as your book is coming together.

Marketing, for example, can never begin too soon. The marketing will be an ongoing effort that should begin right away even if you're still writing, and it will likely continue long after you've published. Marketing shouldn't be an afterthought, but unfortunately that's how many authors deal with it.

It's also a good idea to get a cover designed well before finishing the book, even if you end up making changes before (or after) publishing. A cover helps the project come alive for the author and the readers, though it can be like getting a new hairstyle. You might love it immediately or love it after a few days, or you may decide to make changes. You may even opt for different covers at different retailers as an experiment.

You'll also find it extremely valuable to get editing advice before finishing the writing. Even if you only submit a few chapters to a professional editor or group of skilled beta readers, you'll pick up insights to your writing habits in general, both good and bad habits.

Multitask Along the Way

You'll learn the most about your book and give it a better chance for success if you **work on tasks simultaneously with dedication.** Just as writing takes time, so do many of the tasks related to publishing. There's also a learning curve, especially when it comes to using the internet efficiently, which can be daunting for any writer. Without dedication it's easy to fall behind in your schedule.

To illustrate this point, I've heard from hundreds of writers through my blogs, email, social media sites and video courses, often excited as they prepare to publish. Over the following months to years, I sometimes hear from the same authors who haven't made much progress since the last time we talked. It's understandable as writing is hard, but it's a shame as their stories are being delayed for so long.

I believe most of the authors who struggle the longest to publish are following the list that believes in writing the book entirely first. They do one thing at a time and get stuck at the beginning because writing the book takes the longest. Once stuck, it can seem impossible to generate progress.

If this happens to you, *do other tasks to get unstuck.* Work on the cover design, whether looking for images yourself or talking with someone you've hired. Learn a bit about formatting and apply it to your front matter and chapters. Work with an editor or beta reader on your book's description, which will be essential for marketing. Doing other things is a great way to get unstuck and stay dedicated to the overall mission: your book published well.

Prepare for other parts of publishing like you would for writing. Set aside time and limit distractions. Turn off email, cell phones and social media alerts. Get your tea, coffee, music and whatever helps you write. Commit to sitting down (or standing) and working for a certain amount of time and hopefully beyond. Then stick to it.

Everything you do related to your book deserves time and energy. Give appropriately.

In the same manner of doing multiple tasks simultaneously, the chapters of this book are not designed to be followed in chronological order. Feel free to jump around and read chapters that capture your attention first. My advice is to **skim through the entire book,** then decide which parts are most timely for your needs. This will help you determine the grand scheme of things for your publishing world.

ISBN

ISBN is for International Standard Book Number, issued by a select agency in the nation where the publisher resides. You're probably familiar with 10 or 13 digit ISBNs appearing on the copyright page or above the barcode on the back of a print version book. The barcode just identifies the ISBN and may or may not include a price. Even though ISBN is a number corresponding to a book, it has more to do with the publisher and edition than the title and author. For example, the same ebook could have several ISBNs for different retailers selling it, and it would need another ISBN for a paperback version and yet another for a hardcover or audio book. A separate version is needed for the ePub file compared to the mobi file. Even if you change the trim size of a paperback, like from 5 x 8 inches to 6 x 9 inches, it will need a new ISBN.

The main exceptions are for reprintings or minor updates, which do not need new ISBNs. In most cases you don't need a new ISBN for title, metadata, cover or price changes. Since it's an international designation there are varying aspects from nation to nation, so your situation may differ from an author in another country. In a nutshell, if your book is to be sold through a retailer, it needs an ISBN to identify the publisher and edition.

However, many retailers don't require you to provide an ISBN. Amazon, for instance, assigns its own version called an ASIN (Amazon Standard Identification Number). Amazon currently doesn't list an ISBN on the product page even if you provide one, though you can find specific titles there by searching for the ISBN number. If you provide an ISBN to Barnes & Noble, you'll be required to make it specifically for NOOK. Barnes & Noble support said this when asked about ISBNs: *NOOK Press does not check the Bowker status or title assignment of an ISBN that is submitted to a NOOK Press Project. If you choose to enter an ISBN for a Project in your NOOK Press account, that ISBN will be displayed in your sales report, and is not used for any other purpose.* Kobo says: *You will still be able to publish your book on Kobo without an ISBN and sell in over 190 countries worldwide as we will issue our own identifier number when it goes on our site.*

Since most retailers don't require you to provide an ISBN for ebooks, they'll assign a unique one at no charge. The main catch is, depending on the retailer, you may not be listed as the publisher. In the cases of Smashwords and CreateSpace, accepting their free ISBNs will list them as the publisher, not you. You'll still be listed as the author of course, but if you wanted your name or publishing imprint to be listed as publisher, you'll usually need to purchase and provide your own. A few retailers, like Kobo, have certain distribution partners that may not receive your book without a provided ISBN.

This decision divides authors based on specifics, goals and finances. Some authors insist on providing ISBNs while others have never paid for one. Another author might purchase an ISBN for one title (or retailer) but not for another. It's up to you as there are several ways to manage this. Fortunately your book can be successful regardless of how you handle ISBNs.

If you decide to buy one or a pack of ISBNs, check with your nation for the agency that distributes them. You can get more info at the International ISBN Agency: https://www.isbn-international.org/. In the United States and Australia, R.R. Bowker is the exclusive ISBN agency. Prices start at $125 for a single ISBN, $295 for a 10-pack, $575 for a 100-pack and $1,000 for 1,000. As you can imagine, an author with several titles existing in a few formats uploaded to multiple retailers might need more than 10 ISBNs, so going this route can get expensive. Even if you only have one book but plan to sell at multiple retailers and make print or audio versions, then you may want several ISBNs.

Whether or not to purchase ISBNs has been debated since free was an option. The main benefit to purchasing an ISBN is to have your name or publishing imprint listed as the publisher instead of Smashwords or CreateSpace or whichever company supplies your book with a free ISBN. Your book will also have some additional distribution and search-ability factors, though these things are changing rapidly.

In my opinion ISBNs will be most useful to authors who plan to aggressively market print versions (paperback or hardcover) to large bookstores. Ebooks really don't need an ISBN assigned by you because the retailers each have their own way of handling it and will additionally assign their own numbers. If you decide to purchase ISBNs for ebooks, you may need or decide to use a unique one for Amazon and Barnes & Noble while clustering Apple, Google and many other retailers under one ISBN.

Smashwords, the world's largest ebook distributor, sends your book to multiple channels. Smashwords allows you to use your own ISBN or to use one of theirs for free. Vendors like Smashwords and CreateSpace purchase enormous amounts of ISBNs from Bowker at $1 apiece. That's why these companies can offer you an ISBN for free.

Should you buy ISBNs?

If you plan to aggressively market print versions (paperback or hardcover) to large bookstores, then yes. Consider buying ISBNs.

If you are seriously promoting your name, or publishing company or publishing imprint, then yes. Consider buying ISBNs. (A single publishing company may have multiple imprints, with the different imprints used by the publisher to market works to various demographic consumer segments.)

If you believe the initial costs of ISBNs will be offset by additional sales resulting from select distribution partners and search-ability via ISBN, then consider buying ISBNs.

For most other authors, especially those on a tight budget, the freely assigned ISBNs are a great choice. (I have never paid for an ISBN, but that's just one author's choice.)

What about Print Books?

If you get to the point of making print versions, either paperbacks or hardcovers, then ISBNs will be more important to consider. For those on a budget there are still free ISBN solutions from companies like CreateSpace, Amazon's print-on-demand publisher. CreateSpace gives you 4 options of ISBNs, from free to $10 to $99, or you can provide your own. Each option has slightly different features, but with any of them your paperback can be available for purchase in many parts of the world.

There's a myth that says you need to buy an ISBN and list yourself or publishing imprint as the publisher to be successful. Not true. Many incredibly successful indie authors have published with free ISBNs including Hugh Howey, Amanda Hocking and J.A. Konrath.

Copyright

Like ISBN, copyright generates loads of questions since the legalities of it can be complex. In most cases, it's something you'll rarely think about. The tasks for an author to copyright a book are straightforward. If you have any concerns about it, this fact should give some relief;

By writing your book you own the copyright.

In 1886 The Berne Convention for the Protection of Literary and Artistic Works was signed as an international agreement on copyright. Your creation is your intellectual property. Only you have the "right" to "copy" your work and sell it; nobody else has the right to copy your work and sell it.

Your book is automatically under copyright, extending from the time you write it. However, there is a stipulation of proof. You need to commit the work to a readable form *perceptible either directly or with the aid of a machine or device*. Don't just leave it on your computer or mail yourself a certified letter containing a copy of it. *Perceptible* means you've placed your book somewhere so it can potentially be viewed by others whether they view it or not (i.e. online or through an official registration service).

Every retailer requires you to claim copyright as it protects them and you. That's done with one simple check of the "I claim ownership" box during publishing.

Piracy Concerns

Authors frequently ask about the dangers of copyright infringements or theft of their work. While infringements do exist, they are rare and usually do little or no damage. Many authors will find alleged copies of their ebooks for sale at disreputable websites. Fear not. The great majority of book buyers do not shop at those sites because they're often full of malware. Examples of that type of pirating happen all the time, but Google and other search engines are happy to combat it.

My advice when this happens is to do nothing and not worry about it. You might be thinking, *Really, nothing?* It's true, most of my book titles have ended up on these pirated sites yet I seriously doubt many, or any, sales have resulted. Those sites are not where real book buyers shop! I'll continue to do nothing, and I doubt it has hurt me as an author.

If you want to take a more active response, the Digital Millennium Copyright Act (DMCA) was designed to battle common internet infringements. A DMCA takedown notice can be issued to a website by any author claiming copyright infringement. It's a powerful tool that's easy to use. Essentially you send the website manager or online service provide (OSP) a notice that your copyright has been violated on their website, and the OSP is required to remove or disable access to the material in order to avoid being held liable.

To issue a DMCA takedown notice, request the OSP to remove or block the violation and include the following information:

- your signature
- the work that has been violated
- the URLs or pages you want removed
- your contact info

The Register of Copyrights has published a directory of agents online to receive and respond to your DMCA takedown notice: http://www.copyright.gov/onlinesp/list/a_agents.html. You can also contact a lawyer for more serious claims.

During the months while you're working on the book and sending it to others to read, announce your copyright with the symbol: ©. Place that near the beginning of the document, then include the year and your name along with "all rights reserved" or standard phrasing for your nation. The phrase of © 2017 Author Name All Rights Reserved can be added as a line to the beginning of your books and voila, you're protected (actually you already were). You can include any other legal information following the copyright line.

Copyright pages often include text like: *No part of this book may be reproduced or used in any manner without the express written permission of the publisher and/or author.*

There's no rule for exact wording. Other books have examples of copyright text you can alter for your own. If you write fiction, text like this may be helpful: *This is a work of fiction. Names, characters, businesses, places, events and incidents are either the products of the author's imagination or used in a fictitious manner. Any resemblance to actual persons, living or dead, or actual events is purely coincidental.*

Extra Insurance

Copyright infringement can take forms beyond a pirate stealing a book and trying to pass it off as his own. For example, you may write a successful novel with a unique plot structure. Years later someone might publish a nearly identical book with different characters and setting but essentially the same story. In that case, you may be able to sue for copyright infringement and it will help if you have additional sources of protection.

Plenty of methods for protection exist. These are not mandatory but are wise to do and reasonably priced. You can visit the Library of Congress US Copyright Office (http://www.copyright.gov/) and follow the prompts to register a copyright. Below are divisions for other English-speaking nations.

UK Intellectual Property Office:
https://www.gov.uk/government/organisations/intellectual-property-office

Canadian Intellectual Property Office:
http://www.ic.gc.ca/eic/site/cipointernet-internetopic.nsf/eng/Home

Australian Copyright Counsel: http://www.copyright.org.au/

For more info, visit the directory at WIPO (World Intellectual Property Organization): http://www.wipo.int/directory/en/urls.jsp.

Other Ways to Protect Your Work

If you have a blog, post some chapters and a book description. Introduce characters and the plot to your readers. That can be done even while you're writing the book.

One obvious method to broadcast copyright is to publish the book. This gets into "common law" copyright protection. Imagine publishing with Amazon on May 9th of 2017. After that, if anyone tries to steal your book and sell it online, you could contact the retailer or site owner and prove the book is yours. If a future movie gets made based on your story without your consent or awareness, you'll have proof.

Again let me stress **rarely are authors harmed by copyright infringements.** For the vast majority of authors, please don't worry about it too much.

Amazon and the KDP Select Option

Amazon was the first to enable self-publishers to get their books out to a new population of readers. The Kindle was released in November 2007. Since then Amazon has been the ebook leader in many ways, including creating the most tools to help indies sell books. The result: Amazon sells by far the majority of self-published books. This is true for my titles and for most authors I know. The company has also done some controversial things resulting in plenty of enemies, but that's another matter.

Since Amazon is still the king of sales and indie marketing tools, we'll spend more focus on it than any other retailer. There are many great retailers and we'll discuss specifics for them too, but Amazon is the place to start.

Its publishing platform is called KDP, which stands for Kindle Direct Publishing (https://kdp.amazon.com/). It's the website and platform for uploading ebooks, adding info, making changes or updates and keeping track of sales and payments. You'll become familiar with your KDP dashboard during the publishing process. It's very user friendly.

Your 1st Publishing Decision

Here's an interesting aspect: when uploading your book to KDP Amazon, the first thing authors are asked is if they'd like to participate in a program called KDP Select. It's easy to confuse KDP Select for KDP Amazon because the names are so similar.

KDP Amazon is the publishing platform authors use when uploading digital content to sell.

KDP Select is *an optional program* authors may or may not choose to participate in.

KDP Select requires exclusivity to Amazon for a period of 90 days. This means if you participate in KDP Select, you cannot sell your ebook anywhere else other than Amazon. Not at major retailers, not even at your own website. (Note that print versions of the same book are exempt from the clause; it only covers ebooks.) The exclusivity thing is controversial and can be a difficult choice. You'll find authors on both sides of the fence. Since the KDP Select decision is among the first boxes you'll check when uploading to Amazon, **give it forethought.** There are pros and cons to either choice.

The downside is your book can't sell elsewhere for a minimum of 90 days. No selling at Apple, Google, Barnes & Noble and so many other possibilities. That's a huge number of potential readers who won't see your book.

On the other hand, there are benefits you'll be entitled to by enrolling in KDP Select. The benefits presently include:

- your choice of five Free Book Promotion days or the Kindle Countdown Deals option, both of which are designed to create a buzz about your book.
- your book in KU (Kindle Unlimited) and KOLL (Kindle Owners' Lending Library), which give special deals to members while also benefitting the author.
- your share of the KDP Select Global Fund.
- 70% royalty for sales to customers in Japan, India, Brazil and Mexico, instead of the usual 35%.

Take your time with the KDP Select decision. There's no need to decide now. Just be aware this will be a decision before pressing the Publish button. Regardless of your choice with KDP Select, Amazon is a must for selling books. You'll want to upload the best version of your formatted ebook and cover while also creating a complete Amazon Author Central Profile and more. We're going to discuss all of that in detail.

Using Ebook Distributors in Addition to Retailers

Amazon is a great retailer, but ebook distributors will be important if you want maximum reach to potential customers, especially those who don't shop at Amazon. It's my opinion that authors should make their books available to every reader, regardless of where they shop. Distributors are handy because they upload your ebook to many different retailers at once. This can be useful after making updates within your book's interior or to the metadata, which can happen frequently. Instead of you needing to make those updates with each retailer individually, a distributor can handle changes in one motion. And in some cases, distributors are the only way to place your ebook at retailers who haven't enabled direct uploading for self-publishers.

For example, when I began selling ebooks Apple did not enable self-publishers to upload directly. The only way to get my titles for sale on Apple iBooks was to use a distributor. Now Apple has made changes but requires self-publishers to use Apple software during the process. I don't own a Mac and therefore still use a distributor to place my books for sale with Apple.

Distributors make their money either upfront or as a percentage of future sales. Some are "free to use" but take a 10% cut of each sale at affiliated retailers. Others charge a range of prices and offer a range of packages, like an upfront cost in exchange for 100% of net sales royalties to the author. Either type of distribution service is fine depending on your goals and finances. As long as the distributor is well-established and generally liked by its users, it should provide a valuable service.

Smashwords (https://www.smashwords.com/) is the leading distributor for indie authors. It's free to use and has been in business since May 2008, just six months after Amazon introduced the Kindle. Smashwords is a retailer and multiple format converter, which is unique and enables buyers to read books in any format like ePub, mobi, html or pdf. Smashwords also provides author tools including an extensive profile page. (Surprisingly, many retailers do not offer basic tools for self-published authors, like a profile page.)

Even though Smashwords sells ebooks directly, most authors experience 90% of sales through the distribution partners, like Apple and Kobo, than from the Smashwords site itself. Perhaps that will change. Mark Coker, the company CEO, has always been on the cutting edge of digital publishing as an author and an ebook specialist.

Below are the current distribution partners for Smashwords:

- Apple iBooks
- Barnes & Noble
- Kobo
- Inktera (formerly PageFoundry)
- Scribd
- Oyster (acquired by Google, changes happening in 2016)
- Tolino
- Txtr
- Baker & Taylor Blio
- Yuzu

There are also these library channels:

- Library Direct
- Baker & Taylor Axis 360
- Gardners
- OverDrive
- Odilo

That's a big list which grows bigger each year. You can opt-out of distribution to certain retailers if you want.

Smashwords has strict requirements for formatting. It's common for ebooks to be rejected for not passing the "meat-grinder," the automated program that determines if your ebook passes inspection for conversion and distribution. Smashwords requires proper formatting because it wants to ensure your ebook will look great and function well on any reading device after conversion.

Plenty of other distributors exist. Draft2Digital (https://www.draft2digital.com/) is another with a similar business model to Smashwords. The main differences are no formatting requirements and fewer distribution partners, although the main ones are represented. Draft2Digital presently distributes ebooks to:

- Apple iBooks
- Barnes & Noble
- Kobo
- Inktera (formerly PageFoundry)
- Scribd
- Oyster (acquired by Google, changes happening in 2016)
- Tolino
- 24 Symbols

Draft2Digital, or D2D, is like Smashwords in some ways and different in others. D2D does not require any formatting; they will make an ebook with whatever you send them. I find this both a relief and a bit concerning. While it's nice not worrying about technical formatting, the chances of uploading unprofessional looking and functioning ebooks is greater at D2D than Smashwords for this reason.

D2D also has no upfront cost, making its income on 10% of the list price of your ebook sales. If you want, D2D will also format your book for CreateSpace, Amazon's print-on-demand company for paperbacks, though once again there's no formatting requirement. Your paperback may look ridiculous unless you've given them a well-formatted document to begin with.

There are many other distributors, including ones that charge upfront. BookBaby (https://www.bookbaby.com/), for example, is one of the most popular with over 60 retail stores it distributes to including Amazon, Apple, Barnes & Noble, Kobo and other biggies. Beyond BookBaby, there are many companies with services for your publishing needs. If you're considering one of these distributors, remember most of these companies offer "publishing packages," some of which are expensive for what you're getting. Do some homework before signing up for bells and whistles.

Other Major Retailers (Non-Amazon)

Assuming you haven't enrolled in Amazon's KDP Select exclusive program, there are dozens of other retailers you might consider. The largest of them should be on your list, whether you upload directly or use a distributor. Here are some biggies:

- Apple iBooks
- Google Play
- Barnes & Noble
- Kobo

Apple iBooks

Whether you love or hate Apple, the company sells a lot of ebooks. Apple also has a huge global network and loyal customers. You can use a distributor or upload directly, but make sure it's on your list of retailers.

Unfortunately Apple requires authors to use a certain operating system to upload and sell through them. Although you can set up an iTunes Connect account using any computer, you must use Apple's iTunes Producer or iBook Author to set up a title and upload the files. If you don't own a Mac, you have three choices: (1) Use iTunes Producer or iBook Author on somebody else's Mac for this task; (2) Pay somebody to do that for you; (3) Use one of the approved Apple aggregators.

Apple also has an application process. Because of these unique hoops, many authors upload to Apple via a distributor even though Apple does have a direct portal for self-publishers. If you're interested, you'll need an existing and valid Apple ID with your credit card on file and a seller account at iTunes Connect, more ideal for Mac users than PC. More info of how to apply for those interested can be found here: https://www.apple.com/itunes/working-itunes/sell-content/books/.

Google Play

Google is an interesting major retailer because it's the only one that doesn't manufacture a device for reading ebooks. Google, like Apple, has a tremendous global network. In the past I considered Google an optional place to sell ebooks, but that changed when I realized my titles sold better there than at some major retailers. Now I recommend authors to participate in Google's Partner Program (https://play.google.com/books/publish/), the present name for where you upload ebooks to sell on Google Play, the umbrella of digital products that Google retails.

Since I began writing this book, Google Partner Program has temporarily closed to new authors in an effort to reduce cases of piracy. This could change anytime as indicated by this customer support message: *We've temporarily closed new publisher sign ups in the Play Books Partner Center, so we can improve our content management capabilities and our user experience. We're working to reopen this to new publishers soon. Thanks for your patience.*

Google also mentions you may contact them to be informed as soon as they're back to business as normal for new publishers.

Barnes & Noble

For being one of the world's largest bookstores, Barnes & Noble was a bit slow creating a way for self-publishers to upload and sell ebooks directly. Eventually it created one, which is presently called Nook Press (https://www.nookpress.com/), a good addition to your retailer list assuming you're not enrolled in KDP Select. Currently Nook Press is available to authors in the following countries: US, UK, France, Italy, Germany, Spain, The Netherlands and Belgium. Hopefully more will be added in the near future.

Nook Press functions like Amazon's KDP, although it does not have an exclusive sales program. One nice difference is the built-in editor enabling you to edit documents within the Nook system.

Kobo

Kobo is a Canadian outfit, around since December 2009. It has a direct method for uploading called Writing Life (https://writinglife.kobobooks.com/). Like Nook Press, Kobo's Writing Life also has a handy built-in editing system.

Top Strategies for Choosing Retailers and Distributors

There are about 5 intelligent ways to choose which retailers to sell from and how to get your book into their system. **In no particular order,** these methods below represent common options. Depending on your available time, finances and interest in doing things for yourself, any of these options might be best for you and your book.

Option A) Upload to Amazon and enroll in KDP Select. The main pros: simplified life and KDP Select benefits. The main con: you can't sell anywhere else for a minimum of 90 days. This is a good choice if you want to focus solely on Amazon and keep things simple.

Option B) Upload to Amazon, Google and Smashwords. The pros: fairly simple and all retailers covered because of Smashwords distribution partners. The main cons: Smashwords formatting can be tricky and Google can be unreliable.

Option C) Upload to Amazon, Google and Draft2Digital. The pros: fairly simple and the best retailers covered. The con: fewer retailers than Smashwords.

Option D) Upload to Amazon, Apple, Google, Barnes & Noble, Kobo and Smashwords (for its other retail partners). The pros: **every retailer covered and highest royalties on sales.** The con: most labor involved for uploading or making updates in the future. Maybe you discover typos or just want to make additions. Re-submitting your ebook to retailers is free to do but can take substantial time when manually uploading to each retailer. If you have extra time, want to save money and like do-it-yourself projects, this is a great way to go.

Option E) Upload to a paid distributor like BookBaby. The pro: simplified life. The con: usually cost involved upfront, although this could pay off if your books sell well.

If you want to do the least amount of work, Options A and E are smart ways to go.

If you're willing to put in extra time to save money and also maximize your book's exposure, Options B, C and D are fine choices.

Part 3: Editing

The most common complaint from readers about self-published authors is the lack of editing in their books. Some are riddled with typos and bad grammar. Some are plagued with narrative or structural issues. Those "little" things add up, with each instance diminishing the reader's overall enjoyment. No matter how wonderful your story is, if it's not well-edited it won't give readers the full impact it could have. Good editing ensures better reviews, more recommendations to other readers and more sales.

The obvious hurdle for many authors is the cost as editing may be the most expensive investment a writer will make for her book. Fortunately there are options for authors on any budget. In this section we'll discuss beta readers and professional editors. Hopefully you'll find the right mix of both to help your book reach its potential without leaving a gigantic void in your wallet.

Beta Readers

Beta readers see your manuscript before it goes to an editor. They are not trained professionals, but if you find several skilled beta readers, their value cannot be overstated. Think of them like a critique group of avid readers. They'll find typos, awkward phrasing and poor word choice. They may also have brilliant ideas to incorporate into the story or suggestions for altering the narrative.

Professional editors can be expensive. In cases where the author can't afford an editor, beta readers are the best alternative. And for those who can afford an editor, beta readers can still be used since their input will make your manuscript better, thus making the editor's job easier. Some of the reasons beta readers are so valuable:

- they're often free or very affordable
- two heads are better than one, and ten heads are better than two (yours and your editor's)
- they can write reviews once the book is published

Genre Specific

Beta readers who enjoy your genre are preferable to those who don't. If you write science fiction, get readers who enjoy science fiction. Same for young adult romance, memoir or any genre.

Payment

Most beta readers work for free or for a fair trade. Perhaps they read for you and you read for them. However, some authors pay modest amounts for beta readers. Matthew Mather, author of *Cyberstorm,* ran a Craigslist ad asking for beta readers. He found 20 people and paid them $20 apiece. For $400 he received a ton of great feedback, plus the readers recommended his novel to their friends and wrote reviews as soon as it was available at Amazon. It became a bestseller and currently has 5,000 reviews!

How to Find

Your social media circles are great places to connect with potential beta readers. A Facebook group search for beta readers will reveal plenty. Strangers and online acquaintances are usually smarter choices than friends and family since it's easier for strangers to be candid with recommendations. If you also use friends and family, make it clear you need absolute honesty even if it sounds brutal. Pats on the back will not help your book become better. You need to know more than the typos they find; you need suggestions to make your book its best by hearing from others where it's struggling.

Here are a few writing/reading websites that are great places to connect with beta readers:

https://www.goodreads.com/ - try a "beta reader" search there and focus on groups in your genre

http://www.scribophile.com/ - another great option

https://www.wattpad.com/ - primarily fiction (romance, young adult, sci-fi, mystery, etc.)

http://www.meetup.com/ - for writing groups in your area (real people meeting in person!)

http://www.writerscafe.org/

In my opinion, you can't have too many beta readers. Get as many as you can. If you have the means to afford a professional editor, definitely do that too, but after the beta readers have helped you create a better book.

Professional Editors

Editing, editing, editing. This tends to get emotional partly because it involves paying someone to critique your writing, which is an art form. Even though artists need freedom of expression, readers have standards and expectations. It's the editor's job to allow your style to come through while also helping the book meet standards for readers. Editors do much more than point out typos and poor grammar. They find redundancies, fix awkward sentences, limit wordiness and improve the clarity of the manuscript. They know bad writing, great writing and how to transfer the former to the latter. Editors also know readers and specific audiences.

Many indie authors skip professional editing because of cost. Reading with a fine-tooth comb takes time, especially if the editor is assisting in implementing those changes. Finding a competent editor who fits your needs may be difficult, yet it's likely to be the best investment you can make in your book.

How do you find the right editor, one who recognizes your voice, your book's strengths and weaknesses, and helps you find the right balance of those elements at a price you can afford? It can be difficult. My advice is to go with an editor who's interested in your subject matter and has edited similar books if possible. Beyond that, you want an editor who appreciates your style and can improve the delivery of your message. Their recommendations shouldn't *change* your writing so much as *enhance* it. Most editors will work with a small sample of your writing, like the first chapter or several pages from somewhere in the middle. Then you can decide if their work is a fit with your needs.

Levels

Editors often begin by asking what level of editing you're looking for. They'll make recommendations based on a sample, but the final decision may come down to what you can afford. Note that there are varying definitions of the services offered, and many of the duties within one type of editing will overlap to another. My list below may not be exactly the same as that of another writer or professional editor, but for our purposes it should suffice.

Copyediting - looking for "broken rules" and more including typos, grammar, punctuation, syntax, redundancies, inconsistencies and formatting errors. Copyediting has varying degrees of scrutiny (light, medium, heavy) depending on the book's needs and the author's finances.

Line Editing - edits line by line, similar to copyediting with a focus on the rules but also on craft of writing (style, tone, flow, etc.). This is usually the most expensive service.

Developmental/Substantive/Comprehensive editing - focuses on overall content, structure, character and plot, style, voice, pacing, audience and more. These levels often include recommendations to rewrite sections that need improvement with specifics for how to make those changes.

Proofreading - usually considered a final check. This can be the least demanding service for the editor and most affordable. Books ready for proofreading often have been edited to some degree already and are receiving a final inspection.

Where to Find

Finding an editor is challenging, like finding a new place to live. Take your time, ask trusted writers in your social media circles and do some online searches. As mentioned earlier, try to find an editor who likes your subject matter and has worked extensively within your genre. Here are a few websites below, but this list could be much longer.

http://www.thecreativepenn.com/editors/ - Joanna Penn's list

https://www.editorworld.com/
http://www.the-efa.org/
http://www.freelance-editorial-services.com/
http://beyondpaperediting.com/
http://www.editorsforum.org/
http://penultimateword.com/

Part 4: Formatting

An ebook needs to be a file type that can be read by devices or converted at major retailers. We'll focus on the most common formats writers use when uploading to retailers: Microsoft Word, HTML and ePub. MS Word (.doc or .docx) is the most common writing program and nearly every retailer accepts it. However, most retailers convert MS Word to ePub, and so we'll also discuss using Calibre to create ePub files you can upload instead of Word.

I believe every author should learn the basics of ebook formatting. The basics are not difficult. Plus it's enormously helpful if you want to make changes after publishing, which can happen frequently. There are free guides at Amazon and Smashwords designed to make it easier, but if you read the following sections you probably won't need those guides. And if you still don't want to learn formatting, you can always hire out.

Amazon's guide is called, *Building Your Book For Kindle* (http://www.amazon.com/Building-Your-Book-Kindle-ebook/dp/B007URVZJ6/). You don't need a Kindle to read it. Amazon has a free program called Kindle for PC and Kindle for Mac that allows anyone to read Kindle books on their computer, tablet or cell phone (http://www.amazon.com/gp/kindle/pc/download). It's a quick read, though we'll get into details and smart ideas you won't find in the Amazon guide.

For even more info Mark Coker of Smashwords wrote a manual on *universal formatting* since Smashwords takes one document, converts it to multiple file formats and distributes to so many retailers. It's called the *Smashwords Style Guide* (http://www.smashwords.com/books/view/52). The advice within it will help with formatting for any retailer, though let me repeat we will get into details and ideas you won't find it the *Style Guide* either.

Basics and Best Methods

There are two elements when creating ebooks: the interior document and the cover. These are separate items that are uploaded individually to retailers. Because Microsoft Word is the world's most common writing software, nearly every retailer originally designed its system to accommodate Word files. We're going to start there and then branch off for HTML and ePub.

For authors who don't have MS Word, there are free alternatives like LibreOffice (http://www.libreoffice.org/). Many other programs can save a document as a Word file, as with Google Docs. You may also consider purchasing older versions of Word as they are cheaper and still compatible with retailers.

All of the MS Word versions are similar. However, different versions of Word have some items in different locations. In the following chapters some of my descriptions for where things are located may be slightly different for your version of Word. To reduce wordiness, I prefer not to go into specifics for each possible version of Word or Word alternative.

Digital, not Paper

Remember that ebooks function differently than print books. For example, they don't have page numbers. Users have the ability to change the font type and size, plus there are many screen sizes so page numbers mean nothing to ebooks. In general, your document should be **as simple as possible** without a lot of fancy formatting.

Here's a quick checklist of things to keep in mind, and we'll point these out again in the step by step instructions.

- For MS Word, use the Normal Style primarily.

- Use common font sizes, like 11 or 12 for the main text, and use common fonts.
- Get rid of headers or footers, page numbers and page references.
- Do **not** use tabs or spaces for indents. Instead use first line indents or use the block method. We'll explain both of those.
- Don't have more than 3 consecutive paragraph returns. They can create blank screens of ebook pages, especially on smaller screens like a cell phone. Use a manual page break to create a new chapter or anything that starts on the next screen.
- Add images with the Insert feature, not by copying and pasting them in.
- Include a Table of Contents (TOC) with sections and chapter titles. Create hyperlinks in the TOC to go to the proper location in the document when clicked.

These are the main things to keep in mind, but there are plenty more specifics. We'll discuss each as we go through them in the order that most elements appear within an ebook.

I understand that some authors prefer to hire out for formatting. While that's a fine choice, I **seriously recommend** learning formatting even if you plan to hire out. For one, it's pretty easy. But more than that, you may decide to add a simple update or fix a typo in your ebook after it's been published. Tracking down the formatter may become a hassle, and fixing those things will be a snap if you know a little formatting.

For those who prefer not to do it, affordable help can be found at Mark's List at Smashwords for formatting and cover design too (https://www.smashwords.com/list).

Templates exist, where you insert your text in a copy and paste fashion. These templates are often free, provided by people who appreciate donations when possible. DIY Book Formats has free ebook templates (http://www.diybookformats.com/). There are also paid templates at places like Book Design Templates (http://www.bookdesigntemplates.com/).

Another option is to seek out formatters at companies like Fiverr, Freelancer and oDesk. Just visit those sites and type "ebook formatting" or a similar phrase into a job search. Then peruse the results and look for people with plenty of experience and great reviews.

MS Word Settings

Microsoft Word is designed to be dynamic, able to look like anything you want it to. That's terrific for some things but not always helpful when it comes to designing ebooks where you need a basic document that will convert consistently at many retailers. It's best to use Normal Style for the bulk of your interior text. MS Word has preset styles listed in the menu bar, like Normal or Heading 1, and you can modify theirs or create your own.

Normal Style

From the Home Tab, it's usually the first style listed as an option in the menu area above the ruler. A way to check how you're presently using Normal Style is to right-click on the Normal Style box and select Modify. Then you can see the settings that are currently defining it for font type, size, text color, alignment, spacing and indents.

You can modify Normal Style to your own preference, though I recommend a common font and size as mentioned before. For ebooks, I like Times New Roman 12 for my Normal Style, along with left justification and 1.5 spacing. When using a first line indent, I like .25 inches. Those are the settings for this document, just my preferences, but you may select something different for your Normal Style.

To modify your Normal settings right-click on the Normal button, choose Modify and fill in the settings as you prefer, then click OK. Other areas of text that were typed in Normal Style will automatically adjust. You can also highlight a section of text, give it the settings you want for Normal, and then right-click on the Normal button and choose "Update Normal to Match Selection."

Most ebooks are written almost entirely in Normal Style with the exception of pages that are center justified or have special formatting needs like the Title Page, Dedication page, Copyright or other unique page. Heading 1 settings are common for chapter titles, and we'll discuss those more with creating a Table of Contents.

Show/Hide

You'll also want to use the Show/Hide feature. It looks a bit like the Greek letter, pi, although its symbol represents a paragraph return. When you click on the Show/Hide feature (or use CTRL SHIFT *), it displays the formatting behind the scenes. See it from the Home tab next to the Normal Style option in the menu area. Click on it once to make the formatting visible, again to make it invisible. The following two images display the Show/Hide feature in action, the first without it activated and the second with it.

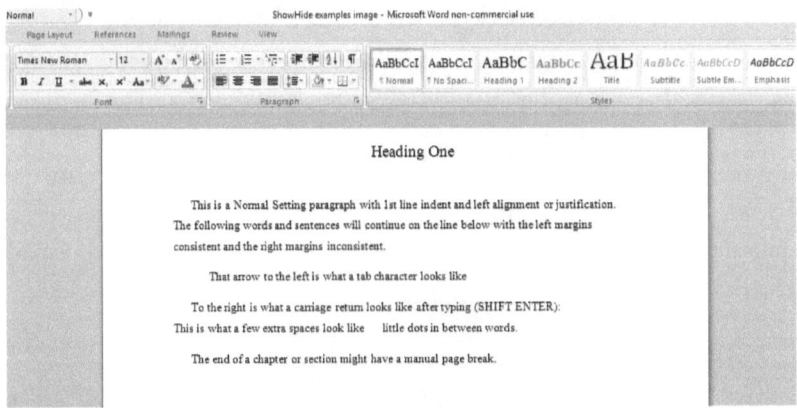

Next see the formatting once the Show/Hide feature is activated.

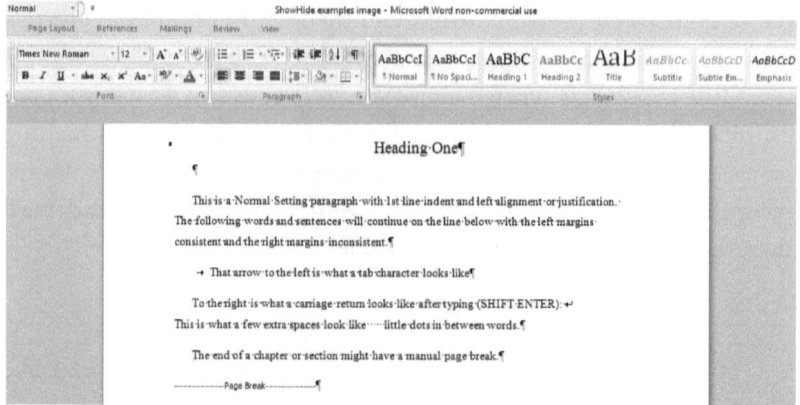

Show/Hide is important for *recognizing and limiting* the formatting elements you've assigned to the document. The main elements you'll see in a well-formatted ebook are:

- a single dot designating Heading 1 setting
- paragraph returns at the end of paragraphs, chapter titles, etc.
- one space between words and after punctuation
- page breaks at the end of chapters or sections

Aside from that, few if any formatting characters should be used. Tabs are not needed. Bullet points sometimes don't convert well, although this document has bullet points. If you use bullets, just use the standard bullet and not a symbol like an arrow or something else, and also be prepared to upload an ePub file as it will probably display the bullets better.

Paragraphs

For your paragraph layout, use either first line indent or block method but not both.

You can set first line indent in two ways. One is to highlight a section and then drag the top arrow of the indent in the ruler bar to the right by .25 to .5 inches. Another way is to click the Page Layout or Paragraph tab, and then choose an indent setting that is between .25 to .5 inches. First line indent is more common in fiction, but many non-fiction books use it too. This book, for example, is non-fiction but uses first line indent. It's your choice as the author.

The other paragraph option is the block method. That's when the first line of a new paragraph drops a bit lower to distinguish it from the previous one. Do not accomplish this by adding an extra return. Block method can be set up with the Page Layout or Paragraph tab and selecting anywhere from 6 to 10 points of trailing space after each paragraph.

Also remember to save changes in your Word document. When saving it the first time or in a different format with Save As, take notice of the Authors, Tags and Title feature that is available. This is your metadata area, and I recommend filling it out. The author name and book title are self-explanatory, but adding tags is related to keywords you'll be using later during the uploading process to retailers. For now think of tags and keywords as individual words or small phrases related to possible book searches (at Amazon) that might lead a customer to your book. Some examples of tags could be: war hero, young adult romance, autism or dog stories.

Front Matter Elements

As mentioned before, there is no single answer for things related to publishing and that includes how you format the front matter of your book. Front matter is everything that comes before the first chapter (i.e. title, copyright, preface, etc.) For a fun thing to do, go to Amazon and **download the free samples** of several bestsellers (http://www.amazon.com/Best-Sellers-Kindle-Store/zgbs/digital-text/). The samples are the first 10% of a Kindle ebook, which will contain the front matter and text from the first chapters. You can read them on your computer, a cell phone, tablet or e-reader. You'll notice many ebooks have different front matter presentations. Some begin with a copyright page, others a reviews section. Some contain a table of contents, others don't. Look at samples to get ideas for how you'd like your layout to look.

Title Page

The title page is often the first thing that appears in an ebook. Most retailers ask you to include a title page. Remember not to include a cover image, as it's a separate file and will be inserted automatically by the retailers. Here's a common way to format the title page:

- Center justify the text.
- Select a large font, like 16 to 22. Type about 3 paragraphs returns into the screen and add the title.
- If there's a subtitle, perhaps make it a bit smaller and type it one or two lines beneath the title.

- Another one or two lines beneath that is a good place for your author name and a paragraph return. (I like my title to be a bit larger than the subtitle, and for that to be a bit larger than the author name.)
- Finally, add a page break by choosing the Insert tab and then Page Break after the last paragraph return to begin a new screen for whatever follows the title page. The following image is an example with the Show/Hide feature on.

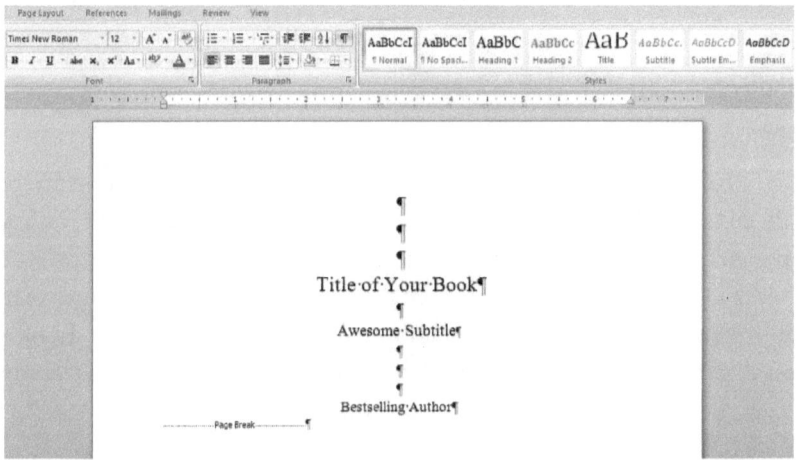

A second option for a Title Page is to insert a graphic or an image instead of text. If you want your title displayed in a fancy font or with additional imagery, inserting it as a graphic would be smart. Kindle won't convert fancy fonts, and it would revert to a font similar to Georgia or not appear at all. You may insert a large image that takes up virtually an entire screen for the title page. It's wise to give some room for error though, since there are many different devices that read Amazon books. I recommend trying a large image, like 6 by 8 inches and testing it in preview mode at retailers first. Next is an example of a fancy font title that was inserted as an image instead of typed.

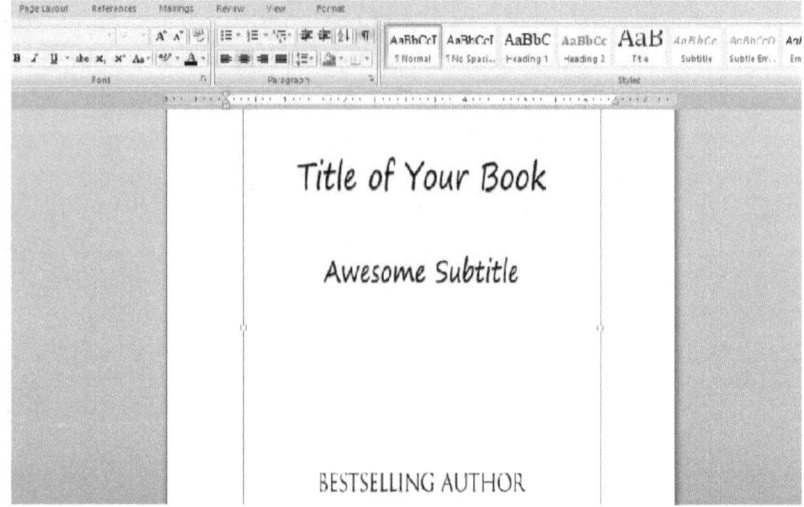

We'll discuss inserting images and using preview mode in more detail soon. Again, you would end this version of a title page with a paragraph return and page break to create a new screen.

Finally, you could create a Title Page Style with a larger font size and "before space" in the paragraph settings. That way your book's title would display lower on the screen without needing as many paragraph returns before the text.

Copyright Page

A copyright page is required and often comes after the title page. Copyright pages are often centered. They need the © symbol and the year of the copyright, which can be typed in Word either by typing (C) without the spaces or by clicking the Insert tab and selecting Symbol and then Copyright. They also need the author's or owner's name. "All Rights Reserved" is commonly found but not required. A simple example that is sufficient would be Copyright © 2015 Author's Name. All Rights Reserved.

If you have pertinent information like an ISBN that you paid for or an LCC (Library of Congress Classification number), it can go there too. Remember that you don't need an ISBN for ebooks, and some authors have them while others don't. If you have legal disclaimers for anything used within your book, those should go here as well along with any text that reduces liability issues.

Copyright pages for fiction often include text like: *This is a work of fiction. Names, characters, businesses, places, events and incidents are either the products of the author's imagination or used in a fictitious manner. Any resemblance to actual persons, living or dead, or actual events is purely coincidental.*

Both fiction and non-fiction often have phrasing like this: *No part of this book may be reproduced or used in any manner without the express written permission of the publisher except for the use of brief quotations in a book review.*

You may want to add contact info, again an optional choice. However you finish the copyright page, follow the text with a paragraph return and a page break to create a new screen. As you can probably tell, this will be a pattern for the end of all sections.

Dedication

Dedication pages can be added like title pages. They are often center justified and lowered by a few paragraph returns before the text, though they are usually a common font size like 11 or 12.

Foreword, Preface, Acknowledgments, Introduction, Prologue, etc.

If you have some of these elements, they're usually formatted the same as text for chapters, which we'll cover after the Table of Contents. An About the Author or Other Books page can either go in the front matter or back matter, where elements after the main body of text go.

For now, check out this list of common **front matter** elements and the order they appear. Remember this is just a suggestion. You can order things differently.

- Reviews, Praise
- Title page
- Copyright page
- Author Bio, Other Books by the Author

- Dedication, Epigraph
- Table of Contents
- List (Figures, Maps, Tables, etc.)
- Foreword, Preface
- Acknowledgments
- Introduction, Prologue
- Chapter One

Amazon Preferred Table of Contents

It's wise to have a Table of Contents (TOC) even if your book doesn't have named chapters, even if you weren't planning to list one. The reason is because a TOC helps readers with navigation options. Beyond that you can list other elements of your book in the TOC, like the About the Author section, and you can create links to those locations. Having a TOC is good for the reader and the author, even for books that might not need one.

We're going to discuss two methods for creating a TOC. One is **specific for Amazon Kindle,** and the other is a **universal method** that will work at any retailer. For Amazon, the method will rely on creating Heading 1 settings in Word and using the References tab for Inserting Table of Contents. Later when we convert MS Word to ePub, your Amazon method for Table of Contents should work universally at any retailer.

Heading 1 font size should be larger than Normal Style. My Heading 1 settings are for the same font type, Times New Roman, but in size 14 or 16 as opposed to size 12 for Normal Style text. See the next image as an example of a Heading 1 setting for chapter titles.

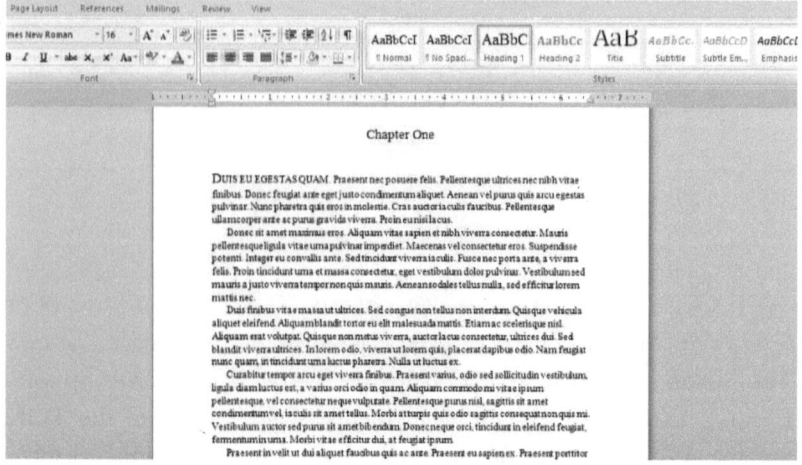

As we did with the Normal Style button, you can adjust and modify the Heading 1 button the same way. Right-click it and select Modify (then choose your settings), or you can highlight a section of text, like Chapter One, modify it to the settings you want for Heading 1 and then right-click the Heading 1 button and choose Update to Match Selection.

All items that are assigned the Heading 1 setting will automatically get placed into the TOC when it gets created with the Amazon method. You should only use Heading 1 settings for those items (e.g. Prologue, Chapter One, About the Author).

To create an Amazon preferred TOC:

- Begin a new screen and type in "Table of Contents." Follow that with a paragraph return.

- Then go through your entire document and assign Heading 1 settings to each section title you want to appear in the TOC. For instance, you might assign Heading 1 settings to the Acknowledgments, Introduction, Chapter One and every chapter title.

- Once those have been assigned Heading 1 settings, return to the TOC page and click the cursor on the next line beneath the "Table of Contents" text.

- Click the References tab and choose Table of Contents and Insert.
- Uncheck the book that says "Show Page Numbers."
- Adjust the box that says "Show Levels" to 1 until it has Heading 1 displayed in the preview. Click OK and see your TOC instantly filled by the items assigned with Heading 1 settings.

Those are now active hyperlinks. If you click on them while holding the control (CTRL) or command (CMD) button, the cursor will zoom to that location as it also will for a future reader of your ebook.

It's important to set a bookmark for the TOC that will become a Kindle menu option for readers. Do this by placing the cursor in front of the "Table of Contents" text and adding a bookmark. On the Insert tab select Bookmark and type the letters *toc* into the box and Add. Now readers will easily find the TOC and use it to zoom to sections within the ebook. (You can insert a similar bookmark, *start*, where you want the average reader to begin your book during a sample viewing.)

If you ever add a new section after creating the TOC, you can select the section title to Heading 1 settings, then return to the TOC and place your cursor anywhere within it. Press the F9 key to automatically update the TOC to include all your H1 settings, including any additions or subtractions.

Universal Table of Contents

The other way for creating a TOC is more universal. This is a fine method for your Smashwords version and for many other retailers, plus it will also work on Amazon devices. The Universal method is done by manually typing the section titles into the Table of Contents, then inserting a Bookmark at the desired location, then inserting a hyperlink from the TOC to the Bookmark.

For example, go throughout your document and place the cursor before each section title, like Chapter One.

- Select Insert and Bookmark and name it without spaces between words or special characters (e.g. ChapterOne). Click Add.

- Return to the TOC and highlight the text for Chapter One.

- Select Insert then Hyperlink then Place in This Document and choose the bookmark you just created.

- Now try clicking on it from the TOC (hold the CTRL or CMD button down while you click) and see if it zooms to that location. Do that for each section within the TOC.

Smashwords uploads are required to have NCX files (Navigation Control for XML), and they can be tricky for new authors to format correctly the first time. NCX is a complex name for a menu option that allows readers to find the TOC on e-reading device (like tablets). Fear not, you don't need computer coding to create this file. It will be automatically created by using consistency with phrasing in both the TOC and at the location later in the book. For example, *Chapter 1: Tequila Sunrise* is phrasing that can be in the TOC and also at the location where that chapter begins with those exact same words, *Chapter 1: Tequila Sunrise*. ePub sellers like Barnes & Noble and Apple will create a user-friendly table of contents as a menu option for documents that have this NCX file.

A savvy student might realize it's smart to have at least two slightly different versions of your document: one for Amazon, one for Smashwords and perhaps one for direct upload to B&N or Kobo. That's what I do, and we'll discuss a few other subtle differences when we mention the other retailers soon.

Chapter Text

Now let's work with the individual chapters. Believe it or not, much of the formatting work is already done.

Starting at chapter one, the first line of text should be at the very top or second line of the screen after a paragraph return. Either way is fine. If you go down much further, it might not convert the same way on e-reading devices as the retailer's conversion software often dismisses extra paragraph returns. Most retailers prefer left justified (left alignment) settings on your end. Don't worry if you want it to look fully justified. The conversion process automatically adjusts for that, and left justified Word documents will upload into fully justified ebooks as you'll see when we get to Preview mode.

Your first chapter title should be in Heading 1 settings. If it isn't already, do that by placing the cursor there or highlighting it and selecting Heading 1. You can update the TOC later as we described with the F9 key for the Amazon method, or by typing the name of the first chapter and adding a location bookmark and hyperlink as in the universal method.

After the chapter title, drop down two paragraph returns where the text will begin. Your text should be in Normal Style with either first line indent or the block method as we described. If you want first line indent, remember not to use tabs but to use the ruler or paragraph feature to set that at .25 to .5 inches. The Show/Hide button will identify any tabs (tabs look like arrows) and you'll want to delete them all. It's your choice whether or not to use first line indent with the very first paragraph of a new chapter. Old school formatting says don't indent the first paragraph, but many authors today do (including me).

I don't recommend inserting a drop cap first letter since they often don't convert well or display consistently on different devices. If you want the first letter or first few words to stand out for aesthetics, you can do that by making them in uppercase or by raising the font size and/or making it bold. That's an individual choice.

Find and Replace

Another handy feature is Find and Replace, useful for making global changes instantly. Let me give examples of the most common needs for this. First, you want to make sure there are not two spaces in a row. Old school publishing was to have two spaces after a period. New school is one, plus you only need one between any words or punctuation. To get rid of extra spaces:

- Click on the Replace tab, and in the Find box click the spacebar twice
- In the Replace box click the spacebar once and select Replace All.

If you didn't start at the beginning or if you had examples with more than two spaces in a row, you may have to repeat the process until they're all gone. Next replace any space after a paragraph return, which would result in the first word of the next paragraph not lining up properly. Click the Replace tab and type ^p (for paragraph return) and the spacebar into the Find box, then in the Replace box type ^p and select Replace All to remove any space after a paragraph return. You can also do that for spaces before paragraph returns, although they won't affect aesthetics as much as the other way. Do a Find and Replace for spacebar and ^p, and Replace All with just ^p. Also note that you can search for specific formatting terms in the Find and Replace feature by clicking More and Special to learn that a Tab Character is designated by ^t, for example. You could then eliminate all instances of tabs by Replacing ^t with nothing.

At the end of your chapter text, finish it off with a paragraph return and a page break as usual. The following chapters will be done the same way.

Remember to add a *start* bookmark either at the beginning of the first chapter, or the Introduction or Prologue, or wherever you want a sample reader to begin. Place the cursor where you want it, click Insert and Bookmark, then type *start* and click Add. Most free book samples will have a reader begin at this *start* bookmark. The location is up to you and can be anywhere in the front matter or at the start of the first chapter. It will also become a Kindle menu option when the reader chooses Go To Beginning.

Inserting Images

Always use the Insert feature when inserting images; do not copy and paste them. JPEG images work great and GIF are fine too. Remember to keep them on a smaller size, typically around 2 to 5 inches in width and 3 to 6 inches in height, like for the About the Author picture. If you want an image that fills the entire screen, you can try as large as a 9 by 11 image in width and height. Be sure to double-check in Preview mode with the knowledge that it might not convert the same on all devices, like iPhones compared to large tablets.

To insert an image:

- Place your cursor on an empty line of text, choose center justification without any indent, then click the Insert tab and choose Picture.

- Find the image from the location on your computer and click Insert.

- You may need to adjust the size of the image by right-clicking on it and selecting Format Picture and Size. Then choose a size as we mentioned. Notice a box that says Lock Aspect Ratio, which will keep the width and height at a constant ratio. If you want to adjust width and height individually, you'll need to uncheck that box.

Also know that aligning images with text wrapping often doesn't convert well. I typically center my images and let the following text come below it, but you can try left or right alignment. When we discuss saving Word as HTML or converting it to ePub, this will help with image alignment.

Common locations for images are in the About the Author chapter, and if you have an Other Books by section and want the covers presented. You may also have images within the chapter text. For books with just a few images, MS Word documents upload well to Amazon, but if there are more images than that you'll want to save as HTML or convert to ePub.

Back Matter, Links and Hidden Bookmarks

As we did for the front matter, the back matter has elements you may want there or elsewhere. It's up to you, but many authors place the About the Author and Other Books pages in the back matter. It seems logical if someone reads your book to the end, they may want to know more about you and your other titles. You can also include a sample chapter of another book. And of course, it's smart to have hyperlinks to your website, blog, social media and other books.

For your About the Author page, I recommend a photo, a brief bio and some links. You'll also want to add it to the TOC as with any section.

- Begin your About the Author page as you would for any new section, with the Heading 1 settings.
- Insert an image as described and set it to a common size, like 2 to 5 inches in width and height.
- Add a brief bio about you. Keep it short and sweet while hitting the good parts.
- Add any social media links and your website for readers to visit.

Hyperlinks

To create an active hyperlink that takes a reader to any site, like your blog, just type out the title of your blog or its URL, then highlight those letters and choose Insert and Hyperlink. Or you can do that by right-clicking on the words and selecting Hyperlink. Paste the entire URL into the box that says Address in the Existing File or Webpage link option, as in http://www.example.com and click OK.

It's best to do that by visiting the webpage and copying the link from the browser instead of retyping it. You'd be amazed how many authors misspell hyperlinks that way. Test the link by holding the CTRL or CMD button down and clicking on it.

I recommend adding a line that says, "Please leave a review." To go one step further, you can add a hyperlink to the URL of the Amazon reviews page for your book after it's been published. Obviously this is something you can only do after the book has been published, but it's an easy update as we'll discuss in the chapter on Uploading to Retailers.

If your reader is still there at the end of book, why not pitch another? And if you have more than one, might as well pitch them all. Like the About the Author page, you could elect to have this material show up in the front or back matter.

The method will be the same: Heading 1 settings for the title. Beneath that insert an image for another book cover. Limit the size to about 2 to 3 inches in height and then add a description under the cover image. If you have several books, you could also make a banner image with each book cover in a row as in the example below.

Delete Hidden Bookmarks

Hidden Bookmarks are additions added by MS Word. They're often added when you insert hyperlinks or elements of navigation in the TOC and then click them to check that they work. When it comes to book formatting, hidden bookmarks can be a nuisance and should be deleted. This is a requirement for Smashwords though Amazon's guide doesn't mention Hidden Bookmarks, but I recommend deleting the ones you don't need for Amazon too.

Check for Hidden Bookmarks in your Word document. The ones that cause problems begin with the letters Hlt followed by a series of numbers. If you have some, it's a great idea to delete them. However, you **need the ones in the TOC,** so don't delete those.

To see what I'm talking about, click the Insert tab and then choose Bookmark. Then check and uncheck the Hidden Bookmarks box. For some reason they don't always show up the first time when you open this. *It's possible your document doesn't have any.* If you see any listed Bookmarks in the box that start with _Hlt and a bunch of numbers, like _Hlt40319955, then delete them. Just don't delete any bookmarks that start with _Toc because those have to do with your Table of Contents. Unfortunately, these hidden bookmarks need to be deleted individually and there can be many of them. They often are associated with URLs to websites and get added just by clicking on the links in your document to check them. If you have links and have clicked on them to see if they work, you may have to recheck to see if any new and unwanted hidden bookmarks have resulted.

The other thing to do is a quick Find and Replace check for the items we discussed earlier, since you may have done some new typing.

And once that's done, your MS Word document is ready to inspect at Amazon. We'll upload and check it in Preview mode soon, but first let's discuss saving this document as HTML Web Page Filtered or ePub for people with more than a few images, or formatting that is a little more complex, or just because they'd like to know how. It is a good idea and only takes a few steps.

Saving Word as HTML Web Page Filtered

If your book has many images, it's wise to save your Word document as HTML Web Page Filtered (or create an ePub as we'll do next). Word documents still upload fine at Amazon, Smashwords and some other retailers, which makes things simple for Word users. Amazon recommends saving Word as HTML for books with any images. I've found it's mostly needed for books with more than 4 images or complex formatting. Either way it's a useful thing to do, and you can test each version of your book in Preview mode to look for any differences. In the past some of my uploads have converted better as Word documents while others have converted better when saved as HTML. Experiment and decide for yourself.

Here's a way to save Word as HTML:

- Create an empty folder that this document is going to be saved to. On your desktop, for example, place your cursor in empty space and right-click, then choose New Folder. Name it something like "HTML Version" to recognize it. Now you have a folder that will be the destination where you save your Word document as HTML format.

- Open your finished MS Word document and click on the Save As feature. Choose Save As and then select Other Formats. Remember to select the destination, which is in the box at the top, as the "HTML Version" folder on your desktop that you just created. In the lower box that says, Save as Type, choose Web Page, Filtered.

- Don't be concerned if Word gives you a couple of warnings like "Saving in this format may remove office tags or features." Go ahead and Save it and then Close the file, which should now exist within the new "HTML Version" folder on your desktop. If you open that folder you'll notice it has two things within it: the text document and another folder that contains the images. If you were inspecting the file, close it now.

- Next create a compressed, zipped file of that folder. Do that by right-clicking on the "HTML Version" folder and scroll down to Send To and choose Compressed (Zipped) Folder. A new folder should appear on your desktop that is nearly identical to the "HTML Version" folder with a little zipper image on it. That entire zipped folder is what we'll upload as the HTML version to Amazon when we get there.

As I mentioned, it's smart to upload both the MS Word document and the HTML version of your book to compare any differences in preview mode. Then you can choose the one you like best.

Making ePub from Word with Calibre

Calibre (pronounced cal-i-ber) is free, open-source software that is a library management system. It's also a really handy tool for self-publishers. Calibre converts documents to a variety of formats and can also check to see how things look on an e-reading device, plus it can edit them. If you don't have it already, you'll need to install it (http://calibre-ebook.com/). Click the Download button and choose your operating type. If you want a longer lesson on using it, type "Calibre Tutorial" into a YouTube search and look for the video from the software's designer, Kovid Goyal (http://youtu.be/Xu_FgtM_Oqs).

Calibre converts to a huge number of formats, but for our purposes the most important format is to ePub. It also lets you edit and add metadata. Calibre allows you to upload in common formats including HTML and MS Word .docx but not .doc. Why? I have no idea so hopefully that will change. If you have it in .doc format, you'll need to convert it to .docx or HTML by choosing Save As then Word Document or HTML. There are many free programs online for converting .doc to .docx if you have a version of Word from 2003 or older, including the free Word alternative known as LibreOffice that we mentioned earlier.

When you open Calibre and are ready to add your Word .docx or HTML for conversion, click the Add Books tab and select your document. Once it has uploaded, you'll have a lot of options in the menu bar for what to do with it.

- One thing to check is the metadata, which you can edit by clicking the Edit Metadata tab.

- If there is a cover image added (sometimes Calibre inserts its own), delete it by choosing Remove in the Change Cover area. You can insert your own book's cover image although most retailers ask for that to be uploaded separately, in which case your book could have two cover images appearing on the first two pages.
- Check your author name, publisher, tags and more. (If you already had inserted tags to your Word document, double-check them as Calibre often doesn't recognize keyword phrases and lists them as individual words.) I recommend adding tags that are related to keywords you'll be using later during the uploading process to retailers. These will be helpful with search engines. Click OK when done.
- Then click the Convert Books tab. Usually the default Output will be ePub, but if it's not just choose ePub in the Output Format tab and click OK. Once it has finished the "job" of converting, you can click the new EPUB link and inspect it.

Note that you can edit the book's content in Calibre by clicking the Edit Book tab. But you can also edit later if needed at Kobo or Barnes & Noble when, and if, you decide to upload directly to those platforms. Each of these choices is fine, but it's good to be prepared for any possibility. The only ePub version that needs to be perfected in Calibre is the one for Google Partner Play since it doesn't accept Word and doesn't have editing enabled.

After clicking the Edit Books tab, editing the new (ePub) document in Calibre has plenty of options. The display will be a split screen of both HTML coding on the left and what the ebook page looks like on the right (see next image). You can double-click on any item in the left side display to select it.

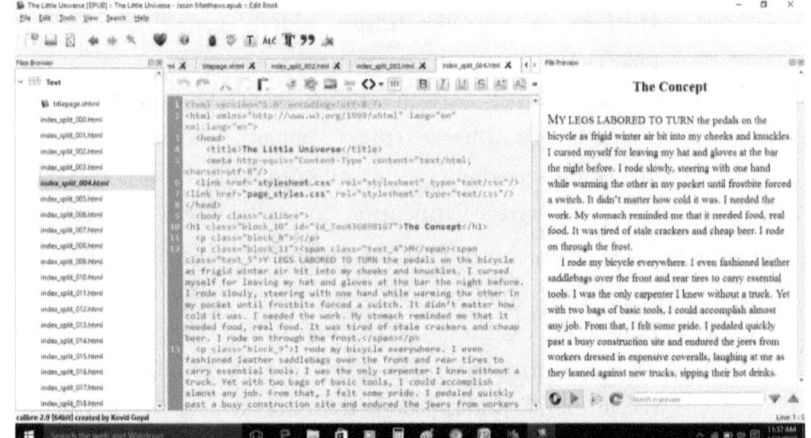

The editing is done on the HTML coding side, but if your document is formatted as we discussed, it shouldn't need much editing. Often I'll just delete the cover image added by Calibre, an easy fix by double-clicking on the first Text section, right-click and choose delete.

When you're happy with the look of your ePub in Calibre, save it by clicking the Save To Disk tab in the menu bar and selecting a destination folder. You can even check the file with EPUB Validator at this web address: http://validator.idpf.org/. It's the same validation service used by Smashwords, Draft2Digital and some other retailers. Just visit the site, click Browse, select your ePub file and Validate. Hopefully it won't have any errors, but if it does they will be listed along with their location to address those issues.

Now you have three file versions of your ebook: one in Word (.doc or .docx), another in HTML Web Page Filtered and the last in ePub. All of these will be useful as you may want to choose which file version you upload to certain retailers when we get to previewing and publishing.

Part 5: Cover Design

Most successful self-published authors hire professionals for cover design. An eye-catching design obviously helps sell books. If you have the means, hire out for a quality cover by someone with work that has sold well. Do not decide frivolously to make your own and do not hire someone without experience.

But even if you do hire out, it's wise to learn about the process. Besides benefitting from knowing more on industry standards, learning to work with images and text will help with everything you do. Since authors do their own marketing, simple graphic design tools will help immensely for things like creating blog posts about subjects within your book.

Before you design a cover, check out the top selling books on Amazon (http://www.amazon.com/gp/bestsellers/books/). Some of the covers of bestsellers may surprise you in their simplicity. It should not only surprise you, but it should inspire you and take a little concern out of wanting the world's greatest cover design. Another benefit to browsing is that it may generate ideas for your book. Look at dozens of covers in your genre, thinking about aspects to adopt for yours.

Standards and Professional Designers

It's important to know retailer expectations and to make sure your designer knows too. Each retailer has its own specifics.

Amazon prefers JPEG (.jpg) or TIFF (.tif) image files, and a 1.6 height to width ratio with minimums of width at 625 pixels and height at 1000 pixels. Amazon's recommended size is 1563 by 2500 pixels. Don't stress if your cover size falls elsewhere. My uploads are typically 1600 by 2400 pixels, which is a 1.5 ratio.

Smashwords prefers JPEG (.jpg) or PNG(.png) files and recommends 1600 by 2400 pixels in width and height. It also reminds authors not to include URLs on the cover or mention other products like "Comes with a free CD!"

Draft2Digital recommends a JPEG 1600 by 2400, but will take any tall rectangle.

Barnes & Noble asks for JPEG or PNG with a file size between 5KB and 2MB, and the width and height at least 750 pixels. For optimum quality, it recommends both the width and height each be 1400 pixels or more.

Kobo asks for JPEG or PNG files under 5MB. The standard Kobo eReader has a screen dimension of 800 pixels in height by 600 in width, which is a 1.333 ratio and equal to 6.67 by 8.89 inches. My covers at 1600/2400 have worked fine there.

Apple requires a minimum of 1,400 pixels and a height greater than the width.

300 DPI or PPI, dots or pixels per inch, is a common minimum recommendation though pixel size is enough to focus on.

1600 width by 2400 height in pixels is a safe **universal** size that works most everywhere, the same ratio as a 6 by 9 book. Also recognize that book covers with white backgrounds tend to fade into the page of a website that also has a white background (Amazon's), so you may consider a thin dark border of a few pixels to "define" a book cover with a white background.

Hiring Pros

When it comes to hiring a professional cover designer, there are a range of options and prices. I recommend talking with several, seeing examples of their work and getting quotes. Prices range from unbelievably affordable to downright expensive. The expensive designers are usually the experienced ones who do the most custom work for you, and prices may run anywhere from a hundred dollars to over a thousand just for an ebook cover. You can find them in many ways including a Google search for "Book Cover Designer," but a better way is by asking for recommendations from writers you know in writing groups. Don't jump into an agreement too quickly. Get examples of their work and feedback from authors who've worked with them.

Mark Coker of Smashwords has a list of affordable, freelance cover designers who do a lot of work. You can see them at https://www.smashwords.com/list.

Some authors hire inexpensive designers through companies like Fiverr, Freelancer, oDesk and Elance, in which case you'll want to do homework to find the right one. It may surprise you to see beautiful book covers made by people who only charge $5 to $25. There are also sites like 99Designs (http://99designs.com/), a crowd-sourced company for graphic design where you can have dozens of people applying for your job by providing covers that you choose from in a contest format.

If you do an internet search for book cover designers, you may find sites like these:

http://www.creativindiecovers.com/
http://www.bookcovercafe.com/book-cover-design/

http://www.jessicabellauthor.com/book-cover-design-services.html

http://myvisionpress.com/

http://archangelink.com/

Do-It-Yourself Methods

For those with graphic design skills and a desire to roll up their sleeves when it comes to making covers, there are plenty of free and affordable tools at your disposal.

Templates

Templates are getting better all the time, providing an affordable yet professional product. Many places have pre-made covers with quality artwork from experienced designers, where you add the book title and author name to existing imagery. Some of these template providers also have deals for creating customized book covers. Let's look at some.

Here's an example where you can add your title and author name into a premade design: http://www.indiebookcovers.blogspot.com/. Or you can contact them for a one-of-a-kind, custom made cover.

Same thing here: http://www.selfpubbookcovers.com/. There are more of these companies doing business each year, getting less expensive and better at what they do.

This one specializes in Romance and is run by Jimmy Thomas, the most photographed Romance genre model in the world: http://www.romancenovelcovers.com/.

Other places for templates include http://diybookcovers.com/ and http://www.bookdesigntemplates.com/bookcover/.

Amazon also has a free cover design template for ebooks called KDP Cover Creator, which is accessible through your dashboard (https://kdp.amazon.com/dashboard). You can provide an image or select one from a gallery of stock images, customizable with a variety of layouts and font sets. If you want to use their templates instead of uploading your own design, choose Design with Cover Creator in section 5, Upload Your Cover. Then follow the prompts for creating one. Editing can always be done later by clicking the Edit My Cover Creator Design button, or you can revert to uploading a cover designed another way.

Let's also mention programs and ideas for those who want to do it yourself the old fashioned way, without a template. This is great info for everyone because *the methods used for making covers can also be used for other things,* like images and text that go into a blog post or social media mention. Once you're familiar with using the tools, it will be a snap to create something that can jazz up a blog post, like this image I made for a post on Foreign Amazons (http://wp.me/pP9sI-19I).

Your Camera

Take photos either of yourself or things related to themes in your book. Many cover images include the author or background landscapes that are just pictures with appropriate text around them. With basic graphic-editing software you can handle additions that will complement your photo. Here's a simple yet effective book cover made by a friend of mine with a photo of a Central Plains home that was a theme of her book.

Public Domain

Public domain is anything not owned by someone with copyright restrictions. Like Open Source, it's free for everyone to use so long as they're not selling it. For a book cover, public domain pictures are fair game. There are websites that offer thousands of free, public domain images like http://www.publicdomainpictures.net/. Just be aware that some photos do require a model or property release, so you'll want to follow through for licensing guidelines.

Creative Commons

Creative Commons or Attribution images are what I use for most blog posts, and I'd also use the right image for a book cover. However, make absolutely sure to contact the photographer or artist and double-check for permission along with proper crediting in the book. Crediting can go on the copyright page. Each image and photographer will have their own conditions, but usually these images are fine for book covers. Just go to a site like http://search.creativecommons.org/ or http://www.flickr.com/creativecommons/ and type in a subject related to your book. Then choose an image and follow up with licensing information. It's best to find the profile page of the artist or photographer and contact them directly by email to obtain permission and crediting information.

Stock Photos

There are websites with millions of royalty-free images for book covers that can usually be purchased for a few dollars. Search the stock photos by keywords to narrow the results, like "big dogs" or "sleeping baby." If you find an image you want and purchase it, then that's fine for a book cover. Royalty-free means you only pay once for the right to use the image on your cover or for marketing the book in general. Here are examples of sites for royalty-free images, and notice that you're likely to find the same image available at several stock photo warehouses.

http://www.bigstockphoto.com/
http://www.istockphoto.com/
http://depositphotos.com/

Image Editing Software

It's smart to get familiar with some photo and image editing software. These products are easier to use and less to install than graphic software. Photo editing might be all you need for creating a simple yet pleasing book cover. Picasa is free, managed by Google and user-friendly (http://picasa.google.com/). Simply download Picasa and follow the prompts. When you want to add images, open Picasa and click the Import button. It will ask from what source and you'll likely choose the Folder option where you can then check the origin and individual photos or entire folders to upload. Check the Upload box, choose your Share options and click Import All. Then you can start editing your images by clicking them to open. Picasa has tutorials for more information as does YouTube.

There is also image editing software, like with Canva (https://www.canva.com/), that is great for book covers. Canva comes with free and inexpensive options. These are some examples of Canva book covers: http://www.pinterest.com/canva/canva-layouts-kindle-book-covers/.

Graphic Editors

Open source image and graphic editors are a bit more complicated but also the most capable. They can alter your images in every way imaginable, and they can also create outstanding images from scratch. Below are two common choices.

Inkscape (http://www.inkscape.org/) makes vector images, higher quality than pixels. I use Inkscape for making book covers and to create images for my sites. Gimp is another common image and graphic editor (http://www.gimp.org/).

If you do-it-yourself, spend quality time and come up with a cover that makes you happy. Remember it doesn't have to be perfect, but you want it as good as it can be. No need to rush through this.

Part 6: Marketing and Author Platform

Writers often ask when they should begin marketing their books. In my opinion the answer is obvious; *marketing should begin as soon as you're certain you are going to publish*. You don't need a set release date or to wait until the writing is finished. All that's needed to effectively market a book is a cover design and description. As we discussed earlier with doing multiple tasks simultaneously, marketing is the one task that can be done during every stage of the process. I recommend you begin marketing **at least a few months** before you believe the book will be ready, and plan on it being an ongoing effort for years to come.

We're only going to skim the surface on marketing. This subject alone could generate many books, let alone a few chapters in this one. Your main opportunities exist online as the internet has created a global community of people sharing ideas. The old cliché is truer than ever; the world is your oyster. You can reach people in any nation and sell books to them especially if you write in English, the most common second-language in the world to non-native speakers. We'll also discuss some offline options for marketing, but most authors market their books with a combination of social media, websites, blogs, forums and email campaigns. You don't have to do all of these and can use them however feels best for you.

Why Wait?

Interesting things happen when you begin discussing the impending release of your book. First and foremost, there's a commitment to the task. Like announcing a diet or exercise program, once you've publicly stated your plans it becomes easier to follow through. Secondly, if people respond with genuine interest, finishing the writing will be that much easier because of their support. And if people do express desire in reading it, some of them may be perspective beta readers who can be invaluable during editing and for leaving reviews at sites like Amazon or Goodreads.

Your Platform Isn't for Diving

Marketing is somewhat synonymous with the term, author platform, which means different things to different people. The two are related but have distinct differences. While marketing is more about the efforts you make to bring people to your book, author platform is more about who you are and what you've done that lends visibility, credibility and reach. I believe author platform is the macro while marketing is the micro; platform is *everything you do and everything about you* that assists with bringing awareness, interest and potential readers to your book.

Author platform includes your past, present and future. For example, if you're writing a book about coaching soccer, your author platform will be strengthened by a history of coaching competitive teams. It would also benefit if you achieve a higher level license for coaching, as in a C license compared to a D license since the C is harder to obtain. But your platform also includes your reach of past and present players, their families, your social media connections, training camps, soccer websites you manage or contribute to, your instructional videos, email list, literally everything you've done or do that gives you **presence, credibility and reach,** all of which may lead readers to your book.

In general, do what you can to consistently strengthen your author platform and to continue to market your book with whatever means you can as we'll discuss in the coming chapters.

Social Media

Social media is a must because it *enables ways to connect with absolute strangers and for them to connect with you.* You need strangers from around the world to find your book, and social media helps accomplish that. It's best to have a **balanced approach,** enough to build platform but not so much that you feel sucked in like you're wasting time. I'm going to share my advice, which you can choose to follow or not.

Step 1. Create profiles anywhere you think there might be value in one. Think of it as planting seeds across a vast cyberspace farmland. Obvious sites include Facebook, Twitter, Google Plus, Goodreads, Amazon Author Central, Smashwords and LinkedIn to name a few. Decide on other sites including YouTube, Pinterest, Tumblr, Instagram, Klout, Quora, and so many more. Recognize that I say *create profiles* and did **not** say *get active daily.* You don't have to visit these places regularly; you just need a profile in place. The reason is because your readers could be at any of these sites and more. By creating profiles there, you give them the opportunity of finding you. For example, one of the biggest directors of traffic to my blog is Pinterest. Am I active at Pinterest? Nope, not at all. But I have a profile there and have pinned a few things in the past, which got picked up by some others and shared and the rest is history. You never know where good fortune will come from, but it can't come unless you plant a seed.

Step 2. Pick your favorite 1 or 2 social media sites and get active. Okay, this time I did say *get active* but kept it to a reasonable amount. Of course you should be somewhat active at a minimum of one social media site. On average, I'm active with only Facebook daily. I use Twitter and Google Plus weekly or so, and YouTube monthly either by adding new videos or responding to comments or questions with my existing videos.

The best way to be active on any social media site is to participate, communicate and socialize.

- share fun stuff you're doing
- share things you find interesting
- comment on other people's posts
- like things
- follow others who follow you (if you like their style)

This light amount of activity doesn't mean you need to be swamped with notifications. You can turn those off in the settings, which I recommend except for the notifications you want. You decide which notifications are important and which to turn off in your settings area for each social media site.

Step 3. Be social. This should be easy to remember because it is *social* media, not a platform to continually broadcast your book is available for sale. You can do that occasionally but not all the time. It gets spammy fast. Treat social media like being at a party with many fascinating guests, and you're a fun person because you talk **with** people, not solely to them about yourself.

Step 4. Create Social Media Icons for your Website and Blog. Make it easy for readers to click on little icons and letters like F and G+ to connect. You can even add these icons within your book so readers can click on the images and connect with you that way. If you'd like a tutorial on how to create your own custom icons and insert them into your site, here's a post on that: http://ourvideoexample.blogspot.com/p/social-media.html.

Step 5. Learn some tips at the sites you most enjoy. For example at Facebook, you may find groups related to your book's subject matter, and then all sorts of networking can happen. When I first released a title on self-publishing, I made a group for it that has grown to over 2,000 members (https://www.facebook.com/groups/110604178950149/). (I believe groups are far more active and interesting than author pages where you attempt to get people to "like" your page, just my opinion.)

On Twitter tag people by including their handle in a post to be sure they get the notification. You can also do a (#) hashtag search for terms people are using related to the post you want to make. For instance, if you've written a book on fighting wildfires, experiment with a Twitter search of #fire, #firefighters and related terms to find the ones being used most often. Hashtags help people find your post, especially those who don't follow you.

At Goodreads, leave reviews of books you've read and comment on other people's comments. Networking with readers is always a good idea.

Step 6. Limit your time on social media. It's easy to waste hours each day if you don't set parameters enabling you to visit briefly but still get other work done. Choose when you visit, maybe in the morning or evening, get your socializing in and return to writing.

As mentioned, we could talk for hours on end about these social media sites. Having more profiles in place to help people find you and your books is always helpful, even if you're not active. Find one or two you most enjoy and spend time there. Do some homework on your favorites and network, network, network.

Websites

I encourage every author to have a website and/or a blog. Even a simple site with a little about you and your books will be useful for any reader interested in learning more or connecting. Obviously your book and social media links should be there.

If you don't want to spend hundreds to thousands of dollars for a professional to make your site, there are places where you can make free sites and blogs like Yola, Webs, Wordpress and Blogger to name a few. Here's one of my free websites: http://your-own-free-website.com/, and it wasn't hard to make. Plus websites and blogs give readers another way of finding your books. The whole point is to enhance your online visibility, your author platform. These sites can contain sample chapters, photos, video and links to retailers.

Domain names are an important consideration before jumping into any website or blog. Do extensive research first. Fiction writers may want to brand their book title or author name. Non-fiction writers may want to brand their subject matter. Homework is mandatory to discover which terms and phrases related to your website title will be actively searched and how much competition from other advertisers exists already.

I recommend using Google Keyword Planner to research the keywords that might be important to your site. This advice is not just for making websites but for research before everything you post online about your book (Amazon description, blog titles, text in the body, YouTube titles, etc.). **Keywords are essential** to help search engines like Google link any Web Page to certain words, terms or phrases. Realize also that YouTube is the world's 2nd largest search engine, and places like Amazon have their own search bars too. It's best to add keywords to every site, blog and location that has boxes for them, keywords that describe the content of what your site and book are about. And you can even figure out ways to include keywords in your domain name.

If you visit Google's Keyword Planner (http://adwords.google.com/keywordplanner), don't worry about their up-selling to get you to pay for ad campaigns. All of your homework can be done for free. Sign into AdWords and click the Search for New Keywords button. Enter a number of keyword terms or phrases (either one word or short phrases) into the box and click Get Ideas and then click Keyword Ideas. Scroll down through the results to get an idea of how frequently those terms are actually being searched by others. Obviously, you want to use terms that are being searched and not completely obscure. But you do want to beware of terms that are so popular, like "weight loss," where competing against the major players might be too large of a battle to win. Look for a nice medium. Instead of "weight loss" you may find terms more niche but still being searched and relevant to your book like "vegan diet," "vegetarian diet" or "vegan weight loss."

Once you've settled on better keywords, consider incorporating them into your domain name for a website or blog.

Blogging

I believe a blog is more important than a static website. Most successful indie authors have a blog and the benefits are numerous. First and foremost, they keep you writing. Writers need that like athletes need exercise. Blogs are also a great way to direct traffic to your books at retailers like Amazon. Readers who enjoy your posts will also see a link for your book and easy-to-click icons for your social media sites. If you post regularly your blog can have excellent SEO factors (search engine optimization), and it might become a top result for search terms that have to do with you, your books and the subject matter of what you write about.

Posts act like perpetual billboards. My blogs still get visitors to articles written years ago like this from 2009: http://www.thebigbangauthor.com/2009/11/edgar-cayce-and-akashic-records.html. Even if you post as infrequently as once a month, your words will be read for years. The potentials are unlimited.

Remember the posts don't have to be the same kind of writing you do for your books. That's why I love my "anything in the universe" blog, where the most popular posts often have nothing to do with the subjects of my books. Some posts are simply subjects I find interesting enough to write about, like the life expectancy of NFL players (http://www.thebigbangauthor.com/2011/10/nfl-players-life-expectancy-might-be.html).

But it wasn't always this way. Back when I first started, I dreaded the thought of having a blog. It sounded like work, and I didn't know how much time it would consume. You may feel the same way. Understandable. My advice is to blog however it fits into your schedule. As a reader, sometimes I prefer short messages with immediate gratification while other times I'm willing to delve into a topic. It's smart to write both ways too.

You may be wondering if blog posts help sell books? My experience has been a mixed bag. My non-fiction blog (http://ebooksuccess4free.wordpress.com/) sells non-fiction books better than my "anything in the universe" blog sells novels. This estimate is based on the number of Amazon links that get clicked by visitors, a helpful stat to monitor. Instead of blogging for the sole purpose of assisting with book sales, focus on building an audience and networking. And if book sales come too, that's an extra bonus.

Blogging Methods that Work

- write about topics that really interest you
- post frequently when possible, or more seldom with quality articles
- do it consistently for years (hey, you're a writer and this is a job)
- make it engaging, ask questions to readers, create polls
- discuss topics that get a range of opinions, even controversial ones
- discuss new topics that people haven't heard much about

What Doesn't Work

- blogging primarily about your books or sample chapters
- writing about your daily happenings, life or family
- posting without much substance just to get something out there

For those getting started and on a tight budget, the free platforms at Wordpress.com and Blogger are fine choices. There's no monthly hosting cost, but it's wise to purchase a custom domain name at around $10-$20 per year. Wordpress.org is different than Wordpress.com and can be confusing. Wordpress.org has free and priced blog templates that you'll need to host elsewhere. Wordpress.com has free blog templates and is also self-hosted. Also many websites have a blog tab or function enabling for you to create a blog and website in one location.

If your pockets are deeper and you'd prefer to hire out, there are website designers all over the world. Find one with examples of sites that have a style you'd like for yours.

Essentials that Benefit Blogs

- links to your social media sites, preferably easy to recognize icons
- links to your books on Amazon and other retailers, preferably icons
- subscription or follow links in two locations, one at the top of the page and another at the end of each post
- social media buttons for retweeting, sharing on Facebook, Google Plus, Pinterest, etc.
- sharing enabled with your social media sites and Goodreads, etc. to display your latest posts as they happen
- navigation to other pages (e.g., About - Contact - Sample My Books), easy to find in two places
- mobile friendly features for cell phone and tablet visitors

Advertising

Aside from social media, blogs and websites, other forms of writing can really help. Submitting articles to other people's blogs as in guest blogging, writing in forums on your topic, articles for online magazines and even press releases are great ways to share info about you and your books. The good news is it doesn't have to take much time. If you do a guest blog post, try to make it somewhere with substantial traffic. Here's an example of a guest post I submitted to TheBookDesigner, which gets great traffic and brings visitors to my sites: http://www.thebookdesigner.com/2014/05/selling-ebooks-on-google-play-the-good-the-bad-and-the-ugly/.

There are many websites featuring new books. Some have paid promotions while others allow for freebies. They're especially useful if you ever do a KDP Select free giveaway, and they also help when you feel like spending in general on a little advertising.

I hesitate to mention paid advertising because Facebook Ads, Pay Per Click via Google or any form of print advertising can get expensive quickly with no results in book sales. However, some people have had success with ads so it should be considered by those with deeper wallets. I believe the smartest places to advertise are in conjunction with readers, such as http://kindlenationdaily.com/, http://www.kboards.com/ and http://digitalbooktoday.com/. Other sites for advertising include Book Bub (https://www.bookbub.com/), Kindle Books and Tips (http://fkbt.com/) and Ereader News Today (http://ereadernewstoday.com/).

There are hundreds of other potential sites for advertising. **Use caution** before spending money anywhere without doing homework to discover if other authors have found them beneficial.

Press releases can really help. There are many companies offering free press release services, or you can pay around $100 or more to get greater exposure from your announcement. These are not supposed to sound like promotions; they're meant to sound like news copy, what's happening and why it's interesting. Two outfits that offer free versions of press releases are pr.com and prlog.org. There are also plenty of paid services including ReleaseWire and PR Newswire among others. If you struggle with this form of writing (as I do) there are also very affordable press release writers at places like Fiverr, Freelancer and oDesk.

Submitting articles can be effective too. Remember to be professional when writing articles and have them polished and of quality content. If this is a method you enjoy, you might want to stick with one location and become something of an expert there, like at Ezine Articles (http://www.ezinearticles.com/).

Author Profiles

Remember to use Amazon's Author Central to make the most of your experience there (https://authorcentral.amazon.com). You'd be surprised how many indie authors don't use it, even though Amazon created this tool to help you to sell as many books as possible for obvious reasons. It amazes me that most retailers don't have a similar thing. No wonder Amazon is the king of sales.

Fill out a complete author profile with biography, photos, video if you have it, and also links to your Twitter and Blog feeds. Note that each Amazon Author Central in foreign countries **needs to be done individually**. They exist for the US, the UK, France, Germany and Japan, and the service should expand to more countries soon. Even though it feels questionable if having these author profiles in foreign countries helps with sales, my books tend to sell more in nations that have this enabled than at ones that don't. These are the links for the other Amazon Author Central nations:

https://authorcentral.amazon.co.uk

https://authorcentral.amazon.de

https://authorcentral.amazon.fr

https://authorcentral.amazon.co.jp

Smashwords has a good profile page for you too, but most other retailers are still developing this, so check in with them and look for updates.

Goodreads is a social media site for avid readers to share books, reviews and more. It's owned by Amazon and also allows you to create an author account while networking with readers. Goodreads is another important profile to set up because it's owned by Amazon.

Once you've completed the process there, this will be your author dashboard link: https://www.goodreads.com/author/dashboard.

I believe other retailers will catch on and begin creating their own versions of author profiles. As they do and as you hear about them, add them to your author profiles list.

Reviews and Critiques

"How can I get reviews for my books?"

It's disheartening to see your book displayed on Amazon with no reviews beside it. Believe me, I know. Been there, done that, no fun. Reviews can be surprisingly difficult to get, and it may take weeks before your first one comes in. Unfortunately the majority of readers don't leave reviews. They either don't want to, don't know how or don't think their opinion matters. It's a shame too because reviews can really help a struggling book.

The most powerful thing you can do is to **ask for reviews.** Ask everywhere possible. Ask friends to read and write one. It's likely some of them have already read your book and would be happy to continue helping. *But caution them not to write overly sweet and gushing reviews since skeptics abound and might be put off.* Ask them to be candid and list items they didn't enjoy to keep it realistic. Tell them to leave any number of stars; it doesn't have to be a 5-star review. 3 and 4-star reviews are fine.

During the editing process, you may have had beta readers read your book. That's a great source for getting reviews since these people have helped already and may be willing to help a little more. Make it easy for them by sending a link to the reviews page.

Leave a mention at the end of your book encouraging readers to write a review. After the book has been published, you can update it with a hyperlink that goes directly to the URL of the reviews page at a certain retailer. You can put it at the very end of the book or in the About the Author section. If a reader gets to the end or reads About the Author, she probably enjoyed your book and might be willing to leave a review, especially if you ask at the right time!

Ask members of your social media circles to write a review. Offer a free book in exchange or offer to give a review for another author as a fair trade.

ARCs are Advanced Reader Copies you can submit to review bloggers prior to publication, but you could also add them as an update afterwards. Those reviews often end up on the book cover, in the description or within the front matter.

There are plenty of reviewers who can be found with a Google search. Some charge money, some don't. Many have a long waiting list while others might be available right away. Because this field is constantly in flux, you'll need to do some searching.

Some authors contact Amazon reviewers directly by email. If you know books that are similar to yours and if they have many reviews, you may contact some of the reviewers explaining you have a similar book and wondering if they'd like a free copy to review. To find out if you can email the reviewer, just click on their Amazon profile to see if they've included an email. Be aware many of the top reviewers get dozens of requests every day.

You can also pay for reviews. In most cases this might be a waste of money, but if your book is a gem waiting to be discovered, this could be a great choice. Since the reviewer is a professional it should be unbiased in every regard. Even if the review is terrific, it might not bump sales very much. Some authors mention they spent several hundred dollars for a terrific review that did nothing for their sales. While there is no guarantee it will help, a good review does lend credibility to a perspective book buyer. Here are a few outfits where you can pay for professional reviews (or submit for free services where offered):

Kirkus Reviews - https://www.kirkusreviews.com/indie/

Publishers Weekly - http://booklife.com/

The Clarion Review - http://www.clarionreview.org/contact-us/submissions/

http://indiereader.com/category/indiereader-library/

http://www.pacificbookreview.com/

https://readersfavorite.com/book-reviews.htm

http://www.bestsellersworld.com/book_review_submission.htm

Now comes the scary part. What if a lot of readers have complaints or simply don't like it? Maybe they mention poor formatting, errors with grammar and typos, or that the story just didn't work for them. Hey, it happens. It's happened to me. I can report with good conscience that not everyone likes my books and that's okay. If a book sells well, it **eventually gets some 1-star reviews** because different people have different tastes.

However, ebooks can be regularly edited and updated. If a dozen typos are discovered (by you or by readers), then those can be fixed and updated immediately. Content of the story and other narrative issues can be harder to work out. For authors who sense that the book simply needs to be better, it will be wise to join some writing critique groups and work on improvements.

Critique Groups

There are plenty of online critique groups you can join. There may also be some local writers who get together monthly to share stories, ideas and suggestions for improvements. These groups can help writers of any level, plus the group experience is a powerful motivator to get things done.

Even Amazon has created an online critique group call Write On (https://writeon.amazon.com/). Amazon describes it as *a community where writers share work-in-progress to get feedback from readers and other writers. Post a chapter. Post a bunch of chapters. Post a paragraph describing the great idea you've just had. You don't need a finished manuscript--just a desire to write, improve, and interact with new readers. Sign up with your Amazon account to start posting stories today (it's completely free.) And all stories you post always belong to you.*

Video

"What have you done with video to assist your writing projects?"

I posed this question in two active Facebook author groups. Hardly anyone responded, leading me to believe they haven't done much with video to support their work. That surprised me because it's easier than ever to share video and because the potentials are amazing.

Most people know the world's largest search engine is Google. Did you know the world's second largest search engine is YouTube? That's right, people do more internet searching on YouTube than with many traditional search engines like Bing. Even though producing an effective video is more difficult than writing a blog post, I believe many authors have overlooked video as a smart medium for marketing their work.

The good news is you don't need to produce top quality videos to benefit. One of my more watched videos can be seen here: https://www.youtube.com/watch?v=V6jIOtakzsw. It's a simple piece about the differences between matte and glossy covers from CreateSpace. People regularly click on it from internet searches. Does this translate to book sales? Maybe, maybe not, but it does support author platform.

It's true my videos haven't received the kind of fanfare I had hoped for. Some barely get watched at all while others get a modest few thousand views on YouTube. None have become a viral sensation, but the results have been encouraging enough to keep going. Should you consider ways to add video to your marketing efforts? If the thought doesn't cause you to wince, here are ways for enabling video to bolster your author platform.

Book Trailers

I posted a nomination board for Best Indie Book Trailers at my blog and received a ton of response. Unfortunately I saw some terrible videos, but there were a few gems plus a lot to discuss on the subject. Many authors created videos that looked promising for the mission of bringing more readers to their books. Here's an example of a book trailer for fiction: http://youtu.be/K4qe70YfRXE. It was made by Samantha Chase for her romance novel, *Wait for Me,* and was an affordable hire-out project done by Animoto. My advice is to make trailers as concise as possible, aiming for 90 seconds or less. If you watch Samantha's, you'll notice she adds a few links and social media mentions, which are smart things to do. An active hyperlink could also be added to the description below the video.

Interviews

A common idea is to conduct an author interview whether it's for your own book or another author's. Google Plus hangouts are great for this since they can become YouTube videos with a few mouse clicks. (Google owns YouTube.) I've done plenty of these and while they are interesting, they don't tend to gather as many views or blog comments as I anticipate. Exceptions include when you have a big name guest, like the interview I did with Hugh Howey, indie superstar.

An interview that received more views was with Shoshanna Evers, who writes erotica. She's not as well known as Howey, but she's good at what she does and happens to be quite attractive. It wouldn't surprise me if that video interview has sold some books.

You'll get more clicks if you upload a custom thumbnail image instead of choosing one of the random moments YouTube gives as a prompt. Those YouTube choices come from set times within the video, but those frames often aren't quality moments, as in a scrunchy face. Upload your choice of image to use as a thumbnail, either a high quality shot of your guest or another eye-catching image.

Doesn't Have to be Writing Related

Having a video that attracts viewers for other reasons than your book can interest people in learning more about you. I learned about Dr. Lani Leary by watching her TEDx talk on her career in hospice, dealing with people as they experienced their final days. Not once in the talk did Dr. Leary mention her book, but I found her illuminating and wanted to know more about her topic. I did a little research and discovered she had a book, which I bought and read.

Even videos that are silly family moments but attract viewers can be wise to share. People may watch your video, find you interesting and start clicking from there. Author platform is about planting seeds for networking. Over time the seeds grow into avenues for people to find your book.

Group Topic Discussion

These are similar to author interviews but I like them more. Topics can be on any subject and help people learn. My topic interviews usually do better when we discuss items most authors deal with: formatting, blogging, SEO, etc. More minds in the room bring out more ideas. Again, Google Plus hangouts that become YouTube videos are well-suited for that. The other nice thing about several authors in a production is that they each have an interest in sharing the video. Each author can post the results to their blog and spread the word better.

Tutorials

These are perfect for non-fiction authors who teach anything, and you don't need a degree in education. My tutorial videos consistently perform better with viewers, blog visitors, comments and sharing. People appreciate it if you've helped them learn, and video is a powerful teaching device.

Not surprisingly, the video education field has grown in leaps and bounds. Sites like Lynda and Udemy attract millions of users. Another bonus when making how-to videos compared to how-to books is that videos can be made in a matter of weeks while books take much longer and cost more. My Udemy courses helped me realize the amount of time and money invested compared to the return was not only better for my videos than books, but far better. If you visit the Udemy site, you'll find thousands of courses for sale and some for free, which might give you ideas for what you could offer.

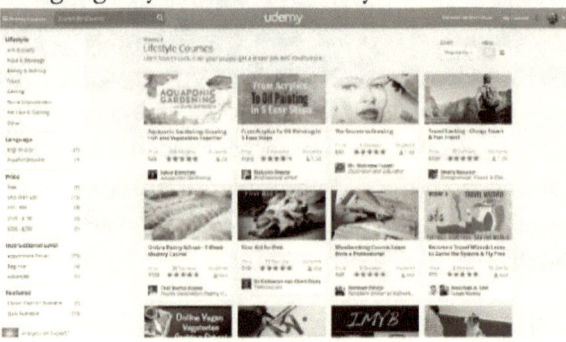

Again, I don't claim to be a Steven Spielberg. If people get value from your videos, then you've got something. Many instructors use Camtasia ($300) for screen capture recording. I use Screencast-o-matic. It's powerful, user-friendly and the pro version is really affordable at $15/year.

Get Creative

We enjoy good videos, probably because we get a sense of who people are quicker when seeing them in action than just by reading their words. That alone may get you to consider making videos, especially if you're charismatic. Remember also that video search is becoming more common on Google. Add strong keywords to titles, and you might do better with SEO in video than for a similar effort with a text post.

As you may have guessed, I've tried many things to market, build author platform and sell books. Call it entrepreneurial, resourceful, you can even call it desperate because all of those are probably fitting. For the most part, I recommend using video with the same *participation theme* that works well on social media. Whenever possible, network and interact without solely broadcasting your own books.

Self-promotion is necessary but should be limited to some degree. Every author has a different style and tolerance level for their amount of self-promotion, so find a balance that works for you.

Email Campaigns

Email marketing efforts are among the oldest methods for promoting products online. For some authors, email lists and newsletters to subscribers are their primary source for generating book sales. Like most marketing tools, these campaigns can work but only if done well over time.

Do not begin an email campaign without committing to it. Plan on several months to years before worthwhile results happen because it takes time to accumulate *interested subscribers*. Email campaigns take much longer than what can be accomplished with a popular blog post, for example, but when done right they can be your #1 marketing tool.

Permission-Based Marketing

Target people who subscribe (or opt-in) to your email list or newsletter. Having a reader's permission to contact them is what separates email from other online efforts. Just be careful not to overwhelm your subscribers with self-promotion, which quickly gives people reason to unsubscribe to updates.

One huge bonus to email: the person on the other end is going to see the subject line of your message. With Twitter, Facebook, blog posts, etc., there is little chance your message will be seen by a majority of your network. Email is the opposite, and so a well-crafted subject line may entice readers to continue on to the rest of the message. Think of that subject line as your best chance to hook a reader. It's got to grab attention with as few words as possible.

Build Audience

The best way to build a subscription list is when readers opt-in to get updates. It's similar to a subscribe or follow button for bloggers. Over time people will give their email if they appreciate what you're sharing. Any method to gain emails is worth trying as long as **people are aware** they're signing up to be on your list. Do not add people just because you have access to their address. That's unethical, plus your messages will come across as spammy if they didn't knowingly sign up. Here are some things you can do to build your opt-in list:

- Pass around an email sign-up at a speaking event.
- Host a contest with a prize like a free book, an hour of your services or even a Kindle tablet.
- Have a subscriber form list with incentives on your website.
- Blog regularly with interesting posts and a newsletter offer in the sidebar or as a pop-up.

When you do contact people, do not simply try to sell your book. Give something of value or help them in some way. Make sure the unsubscribe button is easy to find, preferably one-click unsubscribe, or make it clear how to get off the list for those who've decided they no longer want to hear from you.

Email can be polarizing. Most people don't appreciate a sales pitch in their inbox. How can you keep that from happening to retain more subscribers? It's really a matter of your style and comfort level. Keep in mind how readers might feel as they read your updates.

Frequency

How often can you contact people? This is a two-part question because it depends on how much useful info you have to share while also not annoying the masses. Weekly contact is probably an upper limit (bordering on nuisance) while quarterly is probably a lower limit (ineffective). It's a fine balance, one you may determine through trial and error.

If you're new and want to give it a try, begin by monitoring the emails you receive from other marketers. These should include professional corporations, creative entrepreneurs, even mom-and-pop outfits. How frequently do they contact you? What imagery are they using? What do you like or not like about their emails? Incorporate those lessons to your own efforts. You might opt-in to updates from other authors, especially active ones who have *been there done that* when it comes to email campaigns. See what they're doing that might be good for you to do as well.

What to Include

- blog posts announcements
- updates within your industry
- educational topics for non-fiction authors
- genre related news for fiction authors
- pre-publishing mentions and requests for beta readers
- awards or big news involving your projects

You best results are going to be with a professional service. Some have free versions enabling you to test the waters before committing. Here are a few proven winners:

- iContact
- MailChimp
- Constant Contact
- AWeber

Remember the most important rule: **focus on your subscribers, not you.** Even though you're doing this to assist your own marketing efforts, if the focus is on you and your book, you're likely to have a revolving door of subscribers who leave just as quickly as they came. Figure out ways to add value, entertainment and information to your readers' lives, and they'll be far more likely to support your efforts.

Outside the Box Efforts

It's time to get creative. You may have several marketing ideas that aren't listed in this book. That's great if you do! Coming up with new ideas to sell books is often an author's biggest challenge. My advice is to try anything that seems worthwhile, for you never know what may end up paying off. Stick with what works or feels promising while dumping the efforts that don't.

Local TV and Radio

Most media outlets are constantly looking for material to talk about. Local authors are often considered news-worthy so why not contact the media personnel near you and discuss options for having a news segment? Maybe you'll be on TV, which would be a nice advertising video for your website.

Audio Books with ACX

ACX (https://www.acx.com/) stands for Audiobook Creation Exchange, and they'll help you make an audio version of your book for sale at Amazon, Apple iTunes and Audible.com. If you live in the US or UK, you can find narrators through their site or get tips on recording it yourself. (Hopefully this will open to more authors soon or similar services in other nations.) Some narrators will work for free and split the royalties with you while others work for hire. This can be a huge help to fiction writers since there are fewer audio books to choose from, and many people only have time for fiction when they're driving. Audio books typically sell for higher prices too, so the royalties are better.

Internet Radio Show

There are sites where you can create an internet radio show or be the guest on someone else's program. Hosts are always looking for new subjects to discuss and people to interview. Authors and the subjects of their books are prime candidates to fill air-time. You can also create your own show, interview others with similar interests and subject matter, and create a platform to market your ebook that way. Here are two free internet radio sites:

BlogTalkRadio.com
TalkShoe.com

Host a Show on Google Plus

Earlier I talked about using Google Plus to create YouTube videos for interviews, tutorials, infomercials, etc. It's a great thing to do. Shows can be weekly, monthly or however you prefer them.

Podcasts

A podcast is digital media platform, often in episodes or series. Podcasting is primarily audio files downloaded through web syndication or streamed online to a computer or mobile device. The term is a combination of *iPod* and *broadcast*. Some people prefer to listen to podcasts rather than surf the internet as they drive cars or work out at the gym.

If the thought of producing a series of podcasts excites you, then you'll need the tools for recording audio and a hosting platform for uploading or streaming it for potential listeners. Here are some potential hosts:

https://www.blubrry.com/
https://www.libsyn.com/
https://soundcloud.com/

Video Courses

For non-fiction authors who teach, consider creating a paid (or even free) course and uploading to a video training site like Udemy. These companies use online tools for continued education and are popping up around the world. Instructors can design courses utilizing Power Point, video, screen-casting, PDFs, audio, and zip files. Could authors of fiction use it? Absolutely, especially if you're teaching elements of good writing. Training videos are a great way to establish video presence beyond a simple book trailer at YouTube.

These educational sites offer similar royalties as many ebook retailers like Amazon: free to join and upload courses while paying 70% of any sales to the author/producer. Courses can also be priced free, which might be a smart way to brand or network. The paid lectures typically range from $19 to $99 and more, some are even priced over $1,000.

Foreign Translations

There are translation services and professionals to share your book with foreign readers around the world. Babelcube (http://www.babelcube.com/) is one service that is leading this field, but expect to see more soon. With Babelcube it's free for authors and translators to work together on projects while sharing the royalties of the finished translation. Babelcube handles all the details and uploads to many retailers. You could also hire a translator directly if you think your book might do well in Spanish, for example. Plenty of translators can be found at Fiverr, Freelancer and oDesk.

Crowdfunding Campaigns

Since the world of independent publishing is evolving so quickly, many companies have emerged to help authors achieve their goals and some specialize with finances. It's often called crowdfunding or crowdsourcing, where your project is on display for others to contribute money to help with your needs along the way. Dozens of venues exist for this, and many of these businesses are short-lived. Here are two you may want to check out:

http://www.kickstarter.com/ - Kickstarter funds all types of creative projects, not just books, and does have a fairly involved application process.

http://www.publaunch.com/ - Crowdfunding for books, publishing services and more.

Part 7: Prepping for Retailers

There are a few things to go over before uploading to retailers. The time to publish is drawing near as and you're just about there, but these final things will help bunches.

In this section we'll start by getting familiar with Amazon's preview mode before publishing. Discoveries made there will assist with your final formatting needs. We'll also discuss slight alterations to your document for Smashwords and other retailers and distributors.

We'll explain setting your book up for a preorder so customers can purchase it before it's available for download. For many authors, this will be a wise choice.

And for targeting readers in nations around the world, we'll discuss creating global links that intelligently know where readers live and which retailers they prefer to shop at. That way you won't send a loyal Apple customer to Amazon or vice versa.

Preview Mode at KDP Amazon

You're going to spend a fair amount of time at KDP Amazon in your Dashboard and Bookshelf (https://kdp.amazon.com/). It's important to check the look and functions of your book in Preview Mode, an incredibly useful tool and a fun thing to do. There's no need to wait until the book is finished as you don't need to hit the publish button during the check. You'll probably discover a few things to incorporate into the rest of your writing and formatting.

Another way you can preview how your book will look and function is by uploading it to Calibre. We discussed that as a great way to create ePubs from Word, but Calibre can also be used as an e-reading device similar to a Kindle or tablet. Some of the other retailers also have good preview features while others do not. Of the major retailers, Amazon has always had the best previewer in my opinion.

If you haven't already created an account at Amazon, do that by visiting KDP. Once you've signed in you'll be taken to a Dashboard and the Bookshelf section where you can click the Add New Title button. Then you'll be asked for info including the book's title, subtitle, etc. You'll also be asked if you want to enroll in KDP Select, but don't worry about that now because we're just here to upload your document in both versions and inspect how they look.

Scroll down to the item marked Upload Your Book File. (Recently that was item #5 but now is item #6.) Click the Browse button and select either your MS Word document or your HTML Version Compressed Zipped Folder then wait for the file to upload and convert to Kindle format. Once that has finished, you'll see a new option appear that says Preview Your Book with a Preview Book button. Click on that to open the previewer and get ready to have some fun.

The online previewer is like an actual e-reading device, or devices, as it can be adjusted for different types in the upper right corner. You can choose between the look on a Kindle, an iPad or an iPhone for examples. You can change the font size too, though it's fine to leave it at default settings for our purposes. You can also zoom to a location within the book. Those are smart things to do as you inspect different sections of your document, especially how the Title, TOC, first Chapter and About the Author pages appear. There's also a Go To box that can be clicked and you can choose Beginning, Cover or Table of Contents. The Beginning view will go to the location where you inserted your *start* bookmark, and the Table of Contents will be the TOC or where you inserted your *toc* bookmark. Also notice that your hyperlinks work in Preview mode. Go to your About the Author page and click on your links to check if they go to the proper sites. If a hyperlink doesn't work in Preview Mode, it probably wasn't inserted correctly into Word. It's a good idea to spend a few minutes and scroll through the entire preview making notes for things to adjust.

If needed, return to your MS Word document to make changes. You can then upload the updated document and begin the process again until you're happy with its look and function. Once you're satisfied with the Word document, you may need to save it as HTML again if you plan to upload the HTML version. I like to delete the previous version of the Compressed Zipped File and create a new one to avoid confusion. I've also found with some of my books the MS Word .doc (or .docx) version converts better, and with others the HTML version converts better. Try yours both ways. Remember when you're trying out the HTML version, you'll upload the entire Compressed Zipped folder you created. You may also want to upload the ePub version of your book. Any of those options are fine.

Even though it feels like you're inches away from publishing on Amazon, hold off for now. There's more to it, and you want your best book ready before hitting the publish button.

Smashwords Alterations

Fortunately it's a snap to alter your KDP Amazon document to make it functional at Smashwords though there are a few things to beware of. If your Amazon document is well formatted, it's usually a case of little changes.

The first thing to do is to save your MS Word document with a new name, like *My Book Title Smashwords*. An obvious thing to do yet some authors forget it. Also you may want to make separate folders or figure out how to stay organized since you're likely to have other versions of your book for Barnes & Noble and Google as well.

Smashwords has a requirement for its name to be added to the front matter, usually done on the copyright page. It's as simple as typing **Smashwords Edition,** or Published by Jane Author at Smashwords or Published by Smith Publishers at Smashwords as a single line somewhere on the copyright page.

Smashwords is fussier about Hidden Bookmarks than KDP Amazon so be sure to delete those as we mentioned before. Click on Insert, then Bookmark and check the box for Hidden Bookmarks at least twice because sometimes they don't show up the first time. I know, it's strange.

For the Smashwords version you'll need a Universal Table of Contents, which means you can delete all Hidden Bookmarks including the ones that start with _toc if you have them. Or you can upload a well-formatted ePub (even if your TOC was created the Amazon way).

Smashwords doesn't allow affiliate links or links in the document that go to other retailers. If you had any links in your Other Books By section that went to retailer locations, Amazon for example, those links need to be deleted. Never use affiliate links either because that violates the terms of service (TOS) at Smashwords.

Another thing Smashwords can be a stickler for is having multiple paragraph returns. It frowns on more than a few returns anywhere, and so even for the title page reduce the maximum occurrences of paragraph returns to just two or three.

In the Paragraph settings area make sure there is no number typed into the At box. Check the Paragraph settings for Indents and Line Spacing. The At box should be blank.

The confusing part for most authors is the Table of Contents and NCX file. The free Smashwords *Style Guide* discusses two good methods. The way I recommend, and Mark Coker of Smashwords does too, is a manually linked TOC to each book section as we discussed earlier in the Universal Method. This is **not** the first method I described for Amazon using the References tab, Inserting a Table of Contents and updating with the F9 key. For Smashwords I recommend the second, the Universal Method, of manually typing out each section in the TOC and using Bookmarks and Hyperlinks to make each element active. It is okay to use Heading 1 settings as before, but you'll need to type out the TOC list of chapters and create manual links. Return to the lesson on Universal Table of Contents if needed, or upload an ePub file.

Because Smashwords does not have Digital Rights Management (DRM), or preventatives to keep people from sharing a book, Smashwords recommends adding this at the end of the copyright page: *This ebook is licensed for your personal enjoyment only. This ebook may not be re-sold or given away to other people. Thank you for respecting the hard work of this author.* If your book is free, try this instead: *Thank you for downloading this free ebook. Although this is a free book, it remains the copyrighted property of the author, and may not be reproduced, copied and distributed for commercial or non-commercial purposes. Thank you for your support.*

If you don't mind if it is shared, then don't worry about any of that. I don't believe sharing or piracy is worth worrying about. The more people who share your book because it's so wonderful, the more paying customers will probably support you too.

Smashwords doesn't have the ability to preview until you're ready to publish, so we'll discuss that more in the Smashwords section on uploading to retailers.

Draft2Digital, Kobo, Barnes & Noble, Google Play Alterations

Below are some guidelines for the other retailers. It's usually safer to upload your ePub file or Word document with the universal method for the TOC. Often the Amazon method works fine, but check in preview mode when possible. It's best to delete any Amazon links you may have inserted in the Other Books By section.

As mentioned in the retailer overview, Draft2Digital makes an ebook with whatever you send them. Your Amazon version will work fine there although it's probably better to use a Universal Method for the TOC or to upload an ePub file. D2D will not make any conversions to an ePub though they will make subtle changes to a Word document. D2D does allow you to preview it before publishing.

Kobo's platform, Writing Life, will also accept your Amazon version just fine. Writing Life also has a built-in editor if you need to make changes.

Like Kobo, Barnes & Noble's Nook Press has a built-in editor if needed. The main difference you should make to your B&N Word document is to **change the manual page breaks to section breaks,** as Nook recognizes section breaks for new screens but not the former. This is easy to do with the Find feature but unfortunately not the Replace feature.

- Find the manual page breaks by selecting Find and then typing ^m and Find.
- You'll then need to place your cursor on the page break and delete it

- Click the Page Layout tab then Breaks and choose Section Break Next Page. It's a minor hassle but should only take a few minutes to do them all.

For Google Partner Program, it's recommended to upload both a PDF and an ePub version of your document. The PDF is simple for MS Word conversions; choose the Save As feature and select PDF. The ePub is a bit more involved as we discussed in the chapter on Calibre. Kobo and Barnes & Noble also accept uploads in ePub, as does Smashwords though it previously only accepted Word.

For each of these retailers, you can save a specific document and label them accordingly to avoid confusion. A good method is saving them as *My Book D2D, My Book Kobo,* etc.

Preorders

A preorder is when you arrange for your book to be available for sale at retailers before the customer can actually receive the book. You **do not need a finished manuscript** to make it available for sale as a preorder. Typically you just need a cover design, title and a book description, but if you have a partially finished manuscript you can upload that too.

Customers can purchase your book before you've written one word, which is a pretty crazy concept that can be used to your benefit. Preorders at Amazon are limited to 90 days maximum before the book must be uploaded in its final version. Smashwords allows up to 1 year for the preorder period. Other retailers may or may not allow for preorders, and their time frames will vary.

If you're thinking about going this route, Mark Coker of Smashwords has research suggesting books sold as preorders do better with sales than books sold the traditional way. Coker reports, *"We analyzed Smashwords bestsellers and found that during the prior 12 months, 7 of our top 10 bestselling titles were born as preorders and 67% of our top 200 bestselling titles were born as preorders. Preorders give you a sales advantage!"*

There are attractive benefits to preorders. For one, it gives you a cushion of time to market your book. It also pressures you to finish the book with the incentive of a **very real deadline.** And finally, some retailers will combine the orders received during the preorder period and count them all on the same day the book is actually released, which means your book may rank much higher on the sales charts. When sales spike, good things can happen because more perspective readers see your title at the top of the charts. Your book could make some bestseller lists, and that's more likely to happen when using the preorder function.

Preorder set up isn't mandatory, of course, and your book can be successful no matter which route you take. If you prefer the traditional method of uploading it when it's ready for sale and going from there, that's fine too.

Global Links

Even before publishing, I'd like to mention the wisdom of knowing how to create global links for your books. Although these will need to be created after you publish and once a URL is created for the book or reviews page, it's a good idea to be familiar with what they are and how you'll use them when your book is available for sale. I use these links for all of my books at my websites or wherever marketing my titles.

What are global links and why are they important? Great question. Imagine Jane Reader visits your website, sees your book, wants to buy it, clicks on the link and visits Amazon.com because that's the link you've provided. That's fine if Jane lives in the USA or an Amazon.com affiliated nation. *But what if Jane Reader lives in a foreign country* like Germany, India, Brazil, the UK or a host of other nations where people cannot buy directly from Amazon.com? Or what if Jane prefers to shop at Apple iBooks?

Since you don't know which country your next customer might live in or which retailer she prefers, global links are not only helpful but they may save you from a lost sale. Global links remove the guesswork by determining the nation from the IP address of the reader and the preferred retailer from their history of purchases. Global links can send a buyer to Amazon, Apple or Google, and will probably work for more retailers in the near future.

To see an example of this book using a global link, click the following and please let me know if the link does not take you to your preferred retailer at a nation where you can purchase the book: http://lrd.to/self-publish-to-a-world-of-readers.

These global link programs are ones I have used, but you may find others:

http://booklinker.net/ - only works at Amazon

https://manage.smarturl.it/ - works with most retailers and every nation

https://linkredirector.com/ - works with Amazon, Apple and Google

Part 8: Uploading to Retailers

This is where it gets exciting. It's time to publish at all the major retailers!

Aside from adding a few details during the process, you have everything you need. Just double-check that you have:

- a cover design that fits standards at each retailer
- a well-formatted document saved as Word, HTML Web Page Filtered and/or ePub
- a grasp on Calibre
- a book description that hooks readers
- 7 to 10 keywords or keyword phrases that will help with search engines
- begun marketing with your preferred methods

KDP Amazon

Publishing at Amazon is a user-friendly experience in my opinion. Once you've handled the tasks there, everywhere else will feel somewhat familiar. You'll often copy and paste the same information into boxes at other retailers, like the book's description.

- Sign into your dashboard at KDP (https://kdp.amazon.com/).
- Click on Bookshelf and choose Add New Title.
- This is where you'll enroll in KDP Select or not. It's your choice, and you can return to our discussion on Amazon's *optional* KDP Select program if needed.
- Fill out the boxes for title, subtitle, publisher, etc. You can use your own name as the publisher if you don't have a company. The description is what will appear on the product sales page so it needs to hook readers. Take your time to craft it. Ask other writers in your network for their thoughts. You can make changes later as with almost every element of this process. The Book Contributors box will be for you, the author, and other entities that might need mention such as editor, illustrator, etc.

Note that the ISBN is optional. Even if you already have one, it will only be used for reference. Amazon will **not** list an ISBN on the product page; instead they assign an ASIN to every book, the Amazon Standard Identification Number.

When targeting your book to customers, you'll want to select the two most specific categories. For example, if you write Fiction do not choose General Fiction as a category. There must be something more specific for your book. Always try to get specific while staying relevant to your subject matter. A similar thing happens when selecting 7 keywords, which are single words or short phrases describing your book and content. Keywords help readers find your book by helping Amazon's search engine know what it's about.

Here are examples of 7 keywords to give you ideas for your book: coming of age, romantic, love triangle, broken homes, strong female protagonist, tropical islands. And here are 7 more: doctor memoir, expatriates, Saudi Arabia, alcoholism, medical discoveries, forbidden love, widower romance. Notice how keywords can describe a character, setting, genre, subjects within the book and even the mood.

Also know that some categories exist that don't show up on the categories list at KDP. The way to access them is by using specific keywords Amazon has chosen to correlate to specific categories. To see what I'm talking about visit this link for Selecting Browse Categories (https://kdp.amazon.com/help?topicId=A200PDGPEIQX41). This is where Amazon lists many genres with special categories that can be added only by having a matching keyword. For example, click on the Romance link. Notice that if you wanted your book to be eligible for the special Romance/Holidays category, you would need to use one of these keywords in your choice of 7: Christmas, Thanksgiving, valentine, Halloween, new year. As you can see there are many special categories listed that are not found in the KDP dashboard, so if your genre is among the ones listed on this page you might want to check these out.

Note that even if you select one of the matching keywords for a special category, you'll still need to pick 2 from Amazon's set list and hope your book shows up for the special categories after some sales and getting identified by Amazon. Some authors have success by contacting KDP Support (https://kdp.amazon.com/contact-us) and asking them to add one of the special categories to their book. There's no guarantee, but you can try that too. KDP Support is usually helpful and prompt with responses.

You can choose a release date to either be now or available for **preorder,** which lets customers buy your book up to 90 days before the release date. Even if you choose the preorder option, you'll need to upload a document to pass Amazon's review guidelines. If the document still needs editing, you'll have up to 90 days to get that sorted out and upload the finished version.

Next you can upload your book's cover image by clicking the Browse for Image button and selecting it. Amazon will use that for the product sales page and also insert it into your Kindle ebook.

When choosing whether or not to select Digital Rights Management (DRM), recognize that this **cannot be changed after publishing.** It's basically the only thing that can't be changed. DRM is designed to discourage unauthorized distribution of your ebook, but it has issues and can hinder a buyer's ability to enjoy their book on more than one device. When DRM is **not** enabled, Amazon adds a designation that says *Simultaneous Device Usage: Unlimited.* Here's an example of one of my book's page saying that in the Product Details section: http://mybook.to/LittleUniverse. Some readers look for *Simultaneous Device Usage: Unlimited* when buying. It's your choice, but I recommend not enabling DRM because sales data supports that decision.

Click the Browse button to upload your book file. Here you can choose either the MS Word document (.doc or .docx) or the HTML Web Page Filtered version that is an entire Compressed Zipped File as we discussed. Or you can upload the ePub version. Try each, one at a time, and check the results in Preview Mode. Once the book has uploaded Amazon may prompt you with potential spelling errors in Spell Check. It's a good idea to go through those as they're sometimes correct but not always.

Click the online previewer Preview Book button to activate Preview mode. (You can also use the downloadable Previewer option, but either is fine.) There you can scroll through screens to see how the formatting looks. You can change the type of device by selecting different e-readers in the upper right corner, and you can change the font size. Try the Go To tab to select the Cover, Beginning and Table of Contents. For Kindle devices, the NCX view should also be featured if you created the TOC with the Amazon method. Be sure to check when clicking the Go To button that the Table of Contents bookmark *toc* is working as well as the links to your chapters. Hyperlinks that go to chapters within the document and also to external websites work in Preview mode, like the links to your website or About the Author page. Also try the Go To tab and choose Beginning to make sure it goes to where you inserted the Bookmark *start*.

It's smart to scroll through the entire document to make sure everything looks and functions as you want it. Make notes of changes to make and click Book Details to exit the Previewer. Return to formatting your Word document if needed.

After making changes to your document save it as both Word and HTML Webpage Filtered, and upload the version that worked better in Preview mode. If working with ePub, you may need to revisit Calibre to make alterations. Then return to the KDP Bookshelf and in #6 Upload Your Book File, click the Browse button as before and do the process again until you're happy with the finished product. Returning to this area is also how you would update a newer version in the future after publishing if you need to make changes.

- Once you're happy, click Save and Continue.
- Select your rights. Most authors have Worldwide Rights.
- Choose your price royalty option. If your price is $2.99 to $9.99, you can select 70% royalties as the amount you keep of the sales price. All other price points result in 35% royalties with 99 cents being the lowest pricing option for a List Price.

Choosing a List Price is up to you. It depends on your needs, the quality of the book, your ability to market and so much more. You can change the price later but if you upload to many retailers, changing the price at all of them can be a hassle. If you enrolled in KDP Select, changing the price is quick and easy. Amazon will automatically fill in the corresponding amounts at nations around the world.

- If you have a paperback version and want to participate in Kindle MatchBook, check the box and choose a price.
- If you want to enable Kindle Lending, which I recommend, check that box.
- Finally check the last box and click Save and Publish.

Congratulations! Your book will be available in the Kindle store in about 6 to 12 hours.

Help Readers Leave Reviews

You may remember I mentioned earlier you could add a "Please leave a review" request in the About the Author section. Now that the book is published on Amazon, you could do that by going to the book's review page, copying the URL and inserting that as a hyperlink into the document, then uploading that to KDP as in this example: www.amazon.com/The-Little-Universe-Jason-Matthews-ebook/product-reviews/B00LXGSLJ2/. You can also create hyperlinks that go to the nation where the customer shops. Return to the chapter on Global Links if needed. Anything you can do to encourage reviews is helpful. These updates can be done at Amazon or at any retailer after publishing.

At some point you'll want to click your Account tab and fill in your tax and payment information to receive payments. There is also a Frequently Asked Questions section, and you can also ask questions directly to customer service through the Contact Us tab at the bottom of the page.

Smashwords

Uploading to retailers after Amazon will be a familiar experience with each having minor differences. Because Smashwords is a distributor to many locations you can't get into otherwise, it's a smart place to go next.

After signing in at Smashwords (https://www.smashwords.com/) click the Publish tab. You'll notice most everything is handled the same as it was for Amazon.

One difference is writing a long and a short description of your book. Browsers will see the short description at some sites and the long one at others. In both cases you'll want to craft your best pitch.

You can set your book for any price at Smashwords, including free. This is a rare feature, and the company will still distribute your book to major retailers with that price. Smashwords even has a "let readers determine the price" feature, but I haven't heard a benefit of choosing it. Smashwords has advice on price setting depending on your book and needs: https://www.smashwords.com/about/supportfaq#pricing.

You can also choose the percentage of the free sample. KDP Amazon automatically shows a sample size of 10% of the ebook. At Smashwords you can choose any range and it recommends 15% to 20%.

Choosing Categories and adding Tags will be similar to KDP. Again, get as specific and relevant to your book as possible. At Smashwords you can add 10 tags, which are like keywords (individual words or short phrases).

Smashwords lets you choose which formats your MS Word .doc will get converted to. I recommend choosing each box for every file, even though the majority of people read just a few file types: ePub, PDF, mobi and HTML.

Click Browse and upload for both your book cover and then your MS Word .doc **Smashwords version**, not your KDP version. Smashwords currently does not accept Word .docx, preferring Word .doc. It seems like a trivial difference, but if you work with .docx it's simple to save a copy as .doc.

Unfortunately Smashwords doesn't have a Preview mode before publishing. You check the box to agree to the terms and click the Publish button, then watch everything happen in the conversion process. You only see the outcome after it has published. Your book will then be available for sale at the Smashwords store but it may take a few days to be distributed to retailers. To see the initial conversion results click on the book's product page to download the book in ePub format (or another) and check the book's conversion.

Not to worry if you want to make changes to your MS Word .doc and try again. You can make changes anytime by going to your Dashboard and selecting Upload New Version, which will take you through the process all over.

If you're having trouble getting things to look the way you want, you might try uploading your ePub to Smashwords Direct (https://www.smashwords.com/swdirect). However, Smashwords still recommends most authors to upload in MS Word. If you choose to upload in ePub, Smashwords asks the author to embed the cover image as the first page of the file, which is easy to do with Calibre.

Authors often get a notification that their book did not pass the test for the NCX file. If it happens to you, return to the section of formatting explaining the Universal Method for creating a Table of Contents, and double-check that you have handled it correctly. Also note that Smashwords will require an ISBN for the ebook to get Premium status, but this can be done for free and Smashwords recommends that route. The main difference is that Smashwords will be listed as the publisher.

Once you have passed all tests and been approved for Premium status, you can select which retailers to distribute to. Do this through the Dashboard by clicking the Channel Manager tab (https://www.smashwords.com/dashboard/channelManager/), scroll down and check the boxes either for Opt-Out or Distribute. By default Distribute is selected ahead of time, so you will need to Opt-Out of any retailers you intend to sell from another way, like Kobo or Barnes & Noble if you plan to use their direct methods for uploading. Also notice that Amazon is listed as a distribution partner, but that's misleading since only the very bestselling ebooks qualify.

A nice Smashwords feature is the Profile tab, where you can fill out a profile similar to Amazon's Author Central. Another feature is the Coupon Manager tab (https://www.smashwords.com/dashboard/coupons) where you can create coupons for any percentage off. That's handy if you'd like to give some ebooks away as gifts. The Account tab will have a list of useful items, including your Payment Settings and Tax info that will need to be filled out to receive payments.

Draft2Digital

Technically Draft2Digital is not a retailer. It's a distributor only, but let's mention D2D now because it's a common alternative to Smashwords. D2D has much easier formatting requirements, which is a big plus if you're struggling with formatting. Even though D2D has fewer retail partners, it still gets your book to the big companies like Apple, B&N and Kobo.

When uploading to D2D (https://www.draft2digital.com/), the process will be similar. Sign in, click the My Books tab, the Add New Book tab and fill in the prompts. D2D prefers Word .doc or .docx. It also takes ePub files but won't do any conversion on ePubs, so it needs to be well-formatted if you go that route. (For this reason, I prefer uploading ePub when uploading to D2D. I don't trust its conversion process after seeing poor results.)

Fill in the boxes for Title, Release Date, if it's part of a Series and has a Volume number. The main Contributor will be you, the author, and anyone else who might need mention like an illustrator or editor. You can copy and paste the Amazon description or write a new one. Search Terms will be like keywords or tags. ISBN is optional as it is everywhere, but if you have one specifically for your ebook (not for a print version) it can go there. BISAC categories (Book Industry Standards and Communications) are like the categories at Amazon, and you'll want the most specific choices as your first two. They let you choose five, but some retailers will only list two.

Save and Continue to get to the next page where you'll upload the cover. The main difference is when it asks if you want D2D to auto-generate many items for you, like a Title page, Copyright Page, About the Author page and more. If you have all of those things already in a well-formatted document, do **not** add those again to avoid duplicate content. If you decide you want D2D to add those things, you can always delete them from your document. The choice is yours, but I prefer my own version of these things. Also notice Draft2Digital should have listed your sections in a Table Of Contents manner. Those should match up with your sections and chapters if you formatted as we described before. Save and Continue.

D2D does have a basic preview option before distributing to retailers so you can check to see how things look and make changes if necessary. For most authors, the ePub file for Apple, Nook and Kobo will be the main item to inspect. Scroll through it as you would the Amazon previewer, although it's far simpler than Amazon's. Once you've reviewed it, check the box to approve it for release and click next to choose distribution partners.

Please note it is currently possible to send multiple versions of the same book to different retailers. For example, you could send Barnes & Noble three versions of your book: one from Smashwords, one from D2D and another via direct upload as this example shows when you click *View All Available Formats and Editions:* http://www.barnesandnoble.com/w/how-to-make-market-and-sell-ebooks-all-for-free-jason-matthews/1100667763?ean=2940148369714. I don't recommend this since I've made this mistake before. It will dilute your sales ranking by having sales at multiple locations instead of one. Your book will have a better chance of rising in the sales charts if it has one digital version at each retailer.

Once you've published, Draft2Digital will inform you by email when it has distributed the book to retailers. Make sure to click the My Account tab and fill out the Manage Payment Options to let them know how you want to be paid, either by check, PayPal or Direct Deposit.

Barnes & Noble Nook Press

Sign in at Nook Press to directly upload to B&N (https://www.nookpress.com/). Look for an Ebook Publishing link and click Learn More. Eventually you want the Create A New Project tab. The Project Name doesn't have to be the title of your book.

Nearly everything will be similar but in a different order, with tabs on the side that open to fill in the details. You may upload your manuscript as the first thing, with the recommendation for Word .doc or .docx, HTML or ePub files. You can try these individually to see if you notice any difference in Preview Mode. Remember from the formatting lessons that Barnes & Noble's Nook press uses **section breaks instead of page breaks** to begin new screens. Hyperlinks in your TOC and to external websites should work correctly in Preview Mode. Also you'll find the TOC created the Amazon way, using the Heading 1 settings and the Insert TOC with F9 updates, works fine for Nook Press as does the Universal method.

If you're not happy with the look in Preview Mode, first try making changes to your document and upload again with the Replace Document link. Eventually you may want to try out the main difference at Nook Press compared to KDP Amazon, which is the built-in editing function through the Edit Manuscript tab. This is a great feature.

Click on Edit manuscript. You may notice your chapter headings don't appear as titles but as B&N designations. Those can be individually edited, which can be a royal pain if you have a lot of chapters, but I recommend doing it as Nook readers may see that on their screens. To edit the title of a chapter or section, click on the edit tab to the left of the title and edit. To edit within a chapter or section just put your cursor inside it and edit away. You can do most things you can do in Word, and you can add and edit the size of images, which is something I often do at Nook Press so double-check all your images. You can also click the Preview button from the Editing area to see changes.

When happy, click the Save button and return to the dashboard. There you can fill out the rest of the tabs, which are self-explanatory, and upload your cover image. Little green check-marks will appear next to tabs that have been completed. Again, I don't recommend DRM Encryption, but that's your choice.

You can also add Editorial Reviews written by people with some title or credentials. They aren't required but are great if you have them. It's a good idea to make sure you have permission to use them.

Once that's done, it's time to publish at another retailer. Congratulations! Your profile tab will have a link to your Vendor Account, which will have all the tax and payment info to fill out.

Kobo's Writing Life

Create an account and sign in at Kobo's Writing Life (https://writinglife.kobobooks.com/ebooks#ebooklibrary/authors). Once you make it to the dashboard, click on the Ebooks link and Create New Ebook. By now you should be completely familiar with filling in the blanks, uploading a cover and the manuscript. Kobo will accept your MS Word (.doc or .docx) or ePub file.

As with Nook Press, a TOC created with either the Amazon method or the Universal method should work fine. You can edit with Kobo's built-in feature like at Nook Press. Just click on Edit This Book to edit what you've uploaded. At first glance the look of Kobo's editor may remind you of Calibre's. The sections are on the left while the text appears on the right. However, in this editor you'll be opening a section by clicking on the left and then editing the right side, which is WYSIWYG mode (what you see is what you get), not HTML mode as with Calibre.

When you're happy with the changes, click Stop Editing and follow the rest of the prompts until you Publish the ebook. Congrats again! This is getting easy, isn't it?

Clicking the My Account tab allows you to fill in your payment information.

Google's Partner Play Program

Google Partner Play might be *the strangest* of the retailers you'll encounter. I used to consider it optional for that reason, but since Google does sell a fair number of my books I now recommend it a bit more. Just be prepared for a few potential headaches. Visit Google Play Books Partner Center, sign up and sign in (https://play.google.com/books/publish/).

Google is the only place you'll deal with that doesn't accept MS Word. They're rebels. Instead Google takes ePub and PDF, and it recommends you upload both versions. Through the Book Catalog section choose Add Book and follow the prompts. As with other retailers, ebook ISBNs are optional but you can enter one if you have it.

In the Settings tab choose WORLD for the territories you have rights to, unless that isn't true. It should be true for most everyone.

Another important thing to notice is Google will automatically discount the price you select by about 23%. This is important to be aware of because Amazon will price match your book if it finds it listed elsewhere for less, which has happened to my titles. I recommend boosting your price by at least 25% to avoid the Amazon price match later. For example, if you charge $4.99 for a book and list it at Google, it will be available for about $3.82. In order for it to be listed at the price you want, you may need to price it at about $6.49 to get it to be listed at $4.99. Annoying, isn't it? You may have to play around with the math and the exact pennies.

Once you've done those things, you can publish. Time to celebrate because now you've published everywhere that matters. Nice going!

Click on the Payment Center tab to fill out your payment and tax details.

Print on Demand

For authors who also want print versions of their books, CreateSpace (https://www.createspace.com/) and Ingram Spark (https://www.ingramspark.com/) are the biggest names in the print on demand business. What makes print on demand so attractive are the low upfront costs because there is no minimum number of books to order; books are printed as orders come in so you won't need a garage full of books to keep your printing costs down. You could order one book or one thousand. Or you could order zero books and just let customers order them online directly.

CreateSpace is owned by Amazon. Ingram Spark is part of Ingram Content Group, which also has a division called Lightning Source. Lightning Source is print on demand designed for larger publishers with many books while Ingram Spark is set up for smaller publishers, like most independent authors. The process of uploading to these companies is fairly straightforward for people able to DIY (do-it-yourself), but formatting the interior and handling the cover design for print is more difficult than for ebooks. Most authors will need to hire out to accomplish those tasks, but you can also use templates from places like TheBookDesigner (http://www.bookdesigntemplates.com/template-gallery) for the ease of copying and pasting your text.

Here's an interesting aspect: some authors use CreateSpace, some use Ingram Spark, and others use a combination of the two. Below are the main differences between these companies, which give indications for the option best for you:

- CreateSpace only does paperbacks. Ingram Spark does both paperbacks and hardcover.

- CreateSpace has no set-up fee while Ingram Spark charges $49 per title.
- Amazon integration and shipping within the US are faster with CreateSpace.
- International shipping is faster and cheaper with Ingram Spark, which has printing facilities worldwide.
- In general, authors report CreateSpace is easier to use with better customer service.
- In general, authors report Ingram Spark has slightly better quality.
- You'll need to provide your own ISBN with Ingram Spark. At CreateSpace you can provide your own or use one of theirs for free.
- Bookstores are more likely to stock a book from Ingram Spark than CreateSpace because they get a better discount rate. However, bookstores are unlikely to stock any book from self-published authors unless they are receiving orders for them first.

My recommendation for most authors is to use CreateSpace if the main goal is to have paperback versions available. Also if you live in the US and plan to sell most of your books in the US or through Amazon, then CreateSpace is a good choice.

If you want hardcover editions, Ingram Spark is the way to go. For authors who want to focus on print sales and are willing to take an active role in dealing with bookstore managers, then Ingram Spark will be a better choice. And if you live outside the US or plan to sell many books internationally, then Ingram Spark would be best.

And if you fall somewhere in between, you can always use both of these services for the very same book.

Final Thoughts

If any reader of this book would like a free PDF version that might be handier on her/his computer with all the hyperlinks, just let me know. I don't have any way of verifying who bought the book through a retailer other than if she/he left a review, so if that sounds fair just direct me to the review and receive a PDF copy. Email jason@thelittleuniverse.com with *free pdf for my review* in the subject box.

Now that we've come to the end of this course I want to congratulate you for making it this far. By this point you've written and formatted your ebook. You've learned more about creating a cover and the importance of overseeing the design. You've uploaded to retailers and maybe even made your first sale. What a great accomplishment! I know you'll feel wonderful when you put these elements into place.

I want to ask a small favor. Remember to **celebrate each step along the way** and recognize how special it is. Each of these steps is an accomplishment to be proud of. Don't stress if your book hasn't yet made the bestseller list. It can and you can take steps to get it there. The important thing is that you're doing what you can to give life to your books.

Going forward, remember to be patient. This is not a get-rich-quick scheme. Being successful will require patience, persistence and perseverance to sell books in amounts that make you happy. I hope you'll remember this whenever you're feeling frustrated by the process *as I have felt many, many times.* You're making the effort to share your work with the world, which I think is awesome. Thank you again for your time. Please contact me through my websites if you'd like or if you have questions. I wish you the best of success.

About the Author

Jason Matthews was born in North Carolina in 1967. He graduated from UNC-Chapel Hill in '90 with a degree in film and television. He lives in Pismo Beach, California, where he writes and teaches self-publishing.

He asks readers to please leave reviews at Amazon or anywhere you found the book.

He can be contacted through his websites,

TheLittleUniverse.com - ebooksuccess4free.wordpress.com.

Other Books

The following are available as ebooks and paperbacks at major retailers.

Better You, Better Me - there's a better version of you ready to be energized. The ideas in this book are easy to add to your life, and they work wonders.

The Little Universe - a novel about creating a universe and discovering incredible things within it.

Jim's Life - the sequel novel, about a teenage boy on trial who can see and heal the human light fields, being hailed a miracle healer as the world argues over his case.

How to Make, Market and Sell Ebooks All for Free - self-publish on any budget and sell ebooks at major retailers, your own sites on autopilot and much more.

How to Make Your Own Free Website: And Your Free Blog Too - a how to book for building free websites/blogs and making the most with them.

Get On Google Front Page: SEO Tips for Online Marketing - dedicated to SEO tips, using Google better and rising in search engine rankings.

Sample of *The Little Universe*

Introduction

"WE HAVE SOCIETY! Pinching myself. Yesterday they were primates. Grooming parasites, eating reeds. Today they're driving! Just fifty thousand orbits? How could they evolve so quickly? I need to know. We looked for the link but nothing yet. Possible I missed something, but what? Jim's going over the logs, maybe he'll find it. Mind's a blur—thoughts won't stop—could go on all night. Need to rest, hope I can. Wish Rose could have seen this."

- from p. 66 of Webster's journal.

The Concept

MY LEGS LABORED TO TURN the pedals on the bicycle as frigid winter air bit into my cheeks and knuckles. I cursed myself for leaving my hat and gloves at the bar the night before. I rode slowly, steering with one hand while warming the other in my pocket until frostbite forced a switch. It didn't matter how cold it was. I needed the work. My stomach reminded me that it needed food, real food. It was tired of stale crackers and cheap beer. I rode on through the frost.

I rode my bicycle everywhere. I even fashioned leather saddlebags over the front and rear tires to carry essential tools. I was the only carpenter I knew without a truck. Yet with two bags of basic tools, I could accomplish almost any job. From that, I felt some pride. I pedaled quickly past a busy construction site and endured the jeers from workers dressed in expensive coveralls, laughing at me as they leaned against new trucks, sipping their hot drinks. The aroma of fine coffee made my stomach grumble. I thought of my situation and felt a bit angry.

I wondered if I was a loser. Success meant having things like a good job, a wife and home, kids and pets. I was over thirty and had none of those. I didn't even own a car, but I took pride in limited needs and thought the world would be a better place if more people were like me, common and somewhat content. T-shirts and jeans filled the closet in my apartment, and I liked it that way.

Certainly I wasn't a success. Was I really a loser? It was a good question. The thought was going through my mind as I pulled up, hungry and half-frozen, to his driveway for my first meeting with Webster Adams.

Adams hired me as a handyman. He got my name from his neighbor, an elderly woman who had employed me in the past. He came out to meet me in the driveway, walking quickly in the brisk air, wearing a collar shirt and slacks. He was taller than average, thin and appeared to be late fifties with wavy black hair mixed with streaks of gray. He had very blue eyes.

Adams smiled awkwardly as he surveyed my bicycle. Then he stuck out his hand and shook mine.

"Your hand is freezing," he observed, gripping mine harder than I wanted, not sensing the pain of near frostbite I was experiencing.

I smiled and replied, "Pleasure to meet you, sir. I'm Jon Gruber."

"Interesting transportation, Mr. Gruber. Especially in this weather."

His look was one of admiration and concern. I suspected he was deciding whether he had made a mistake in hiring me.

"Gets me from point A to B," I said, disconnecting the front leather bag. I slung it over my shoulder, hoping to instill some confidence in Adams.

He led me into his house. The entry had a cathedral ceiling with stained glass windows that filled the downstairs with an array of colors, like walking through a rainbow. The wooden floor was finely polished. My footsteps echoed softly as I followed him down the hallway.

"Should I take off my shoes?" I asked. Adams shook his head no.

Dozens of framed pictures hung on the walls of a happy family: man, wife and pretty daughter. The girl instantly caught my eye. Auburn hair, easy smile, the girl-next-door look that I was naturally attracted to.

Adams jogged up the first flight of stairs and I followed. The stairwell contained paintings of planets, nebulas and constellations. Things I knew nothing about back then. Adams paused briefly on the second flight as he passed the largest of the paintings, a massive planet with a purple body and half-finished blue rings around it. It was a lovely piece of work though I wondered why it was unfinished. He stared at it for a moment then continued up.

The top floor was immaculate with marble counters, leather couches and a plush carpet leading to a stone hearth and fireplace where a small fire crackled. I looked around at the trophies of a successful man and wondered if I would ever have those things.

"I want to tear down this wall that separates the kitchen from the great room," Adams explained. "The idea is to make it one big space."

"I can do that."

"Everything?"

"Yeah."

"How would you get the materials here?"

"Delivery."

"What would you recommend?" he asked.

I imagined the finished product and said, "I'll rip out the wallboard and the studs to here, then frame a bar that stretches toward the middle. Then I'll rewire the electrical, texture, paint and whatnot."

He ended by saying, "I want it to be done well, Jon."

I answered with a promise that never failed. "Sir, if you're not delighted with the finished product, you don't have to pay me."

Adams laughed at my guarantee, but a look of ease came to his face. Then he pointed at the counter to a plate full of cookies. "Help yourself," he said. "The neighbor brought them over."

Once he looked away, I took three and stuffed them in my mouth. Fuel for good work, I thought.

I jogged downstairs and grabbed the remaining bag of tools from my bike, anticipating the ride home without the heavy tools or the bitter morning cold. I reminded myself to stop by the Star Bar and pick up my hat and gloves. Samantha would hold them for me. Then I headed back upstairs and began demolishing the wall that enclosed his kitchen. Adams watched me briefly before going to his office.

After destroying the wall, I hauled the debris down to the garage. The place was full of circuits and devices, like a high-tech machine shop. I guessed that Adams was an inventor. He came down and saw me staring at things. He showed me an oscillating microscope and tried to explain how it worked but the concepts were mindboggling. I nodded along dumbly as if I understood what he was saying. Adams didn't seem to realize the information was beyond me as he went on and on with the explanation.

I worked for him for a week. He had a quiet but pleasant nature, introverted. He often seemed absorbed in thought as he came and left frequently during those days, preoccupied with his latest project. Sometimes he would jot notes in a little brown booklet. I heard him mumbling to himself as he read over the notes, complex fragments I could not begin to understand.

"That can't be? Portal from ct over zero at y parsec?" Adams said once in passing.

"Excuse me?" I asked with a paintbrush in hand.

"Sorry, Jon. Just thinking out loud."

"No problem. Let me know if I can help with anything."

He grinned slightly, appreciating my joke.

We couldn't have been much more different. Adams was highly educated and used to wealth while I wasn't. At first we began with the usual chat about weather and sports. Eventually we talked about most anything, especially at lunch, which he preferred to be delivered. We made an odd couple, but we had good talks and laughs and over time I sensed we were becoming friends.

As the job came to a close, I could tell he had something he wanted to ask, but never did I expect what he was about to say. I remember how clueless I felt when he first brought up the subject.

"Jon, have you ever wondered how the universe began?" Adams asked on the final day. He was holding a panel for the bar in place as I set the nails.

"What do you mean?" I asked, continuing to pound away.

"The origin of the stars and planets. Does that *stuff* interest you?"

"A little." I knew we were on a sphere going around the sun once a year and that space was really huge. Beyond that, what was there to think about?

"What do you know about The Big Bang?"

"You mean when the universe started?" I hit the nail but bent it sideways.

146

"Right," Adams said, staring at me. His directness made me slightly uncomfortable, but it was just his way, intense and passionate about his ideas.

"Why do you ask?"

Adams became excited as he spoke. "Imagine watching the universe begin. What if you could go back in time about twenty billion years and see it all happen? Do you have any idea what that would be like?"

"Not exactly."

"It all began with a piece of matter that was infinitely small and infinitely dense." Adams pressed his fingers in a tight spot to convey his message. "Then it exploded in brilliant light! Everything that exists came from that tiny piece of dense matter. Everything! Stars, planets, entire galaxies came from that pinpoint of matter."

"Sounds logical," I said. It didn't, of course. How could everything have started from one tiny spot?

I pounded the last nail and made sure the panel was secure.

"Jon, what would you say if I told you I'm attempting to reproduce The Big Bang? In miniature, of course."

"What do you mean?"

"I'm recreating The Big Bang. Simulating a universe."

"For real?"

Simulate a universe? I knew Adams was an inventor but this seemed impossible.

"Would you like to see the project?"

"Maybe."

"You can stay on the clock if it makes a difference."

I put the hammer down and took off my tool-belt. We left the house and hopped into his truck, a new machine with only a few scuff marks in the bed. Adams drove as he explained the origin of the universe. I listened carefully, but the lecture was way over my head.

We passed the last of the buildings and houses in our town and continued into the countryside for a few minutes. I sat silently, wondering where this project would be and what it would be like.

Adams let the silence extend. Finally, he turned onto a dirt path. We followed it until it ended and arrived at the only dwelling in sight.

"Here it is," he announced.

The Project

IT WAS AN ODD BUILDING way out in the middle of nothing but fields and forest. The structure looked newly built yet it was totally nondescript, unlike anything I had seen in my construction career. The building was three stories high and primarily elliptical, like an oval-shaped frame placed over a rectangular frame. Though it had no windows, it looked finished with a light brown plaster coating the whole thing. There was no paved driveway, just the dirt pad left from the construction vehicles.

Adams swiped a magnetic strip key and pressed buttons for a security code. The tall, heavy doors opened slowly, making a slight creaking sound. I breathed in the scent of new carpet. Large boxes placed on top of the rolls clogged up the entry.

We entered the cool room, leaving the doors open to let in light. The lobby appeared the same as the overall building. It was finished structurally but still needed texture, paint, carpeting and fixtures.

"There's work to do here," Adams said, as he showed me around the lobby. I nodded, thinking the entry alone could use many hours of my services.

Adams flicked a light switch then walked down a corridor to the center of the building. I followed slowly. My attention was drawn to large photos on the walls, dozens of images that must have been taken from a gigantic telescope. Star dust, planets, moons, entire galaxies. They were breathtaking pictures such as I had never seen and in far more detail than the paintings at Adams' home. The matter exploded out from the frames in amazing color. My first impression was that the galaxies were not just rocks and matter, but living things.

"Are these artists' paintings, or are they real?" I asked, tracing my finger around a stellar explosion. The label said it was a supernova.

"They're all real. These are parts of our universe. Except for this one." He pointed to a photo labeled a spiral galaxy. The stars were tiny points of bright light swirling in dark space. "This one's a computer simulation of our galaxy."

"Why a simulation?"

"We don't have cameras far enough out in space to shoot it from this perspective."

"Oh." I felt stupid for asking and reminded myself to keep quiet.

"That's our sun," he added, pointing to a secluded dot way out on a spiral arm of the galaxy.

"That's our sun?" I asked, mesmerized by it.

"That's it."

"What about all these other lights?"

"They're other suns. Some of them are stars you see on a clear night."

Adams opened a door to the main room on the lower floor. We entered a command central with desks, chairs, computer equipment and dozens of large monitors. Some were attached to the walls, and some were still in boxes. Packing foam, shipping plastic and empty cartons littered the floor. On the desks, papers were scattered about. I looked at them and saw handwritten equations. Chemistry or physics, I guessed. They were light years ahead of my understanding. I walked around the cool, dimly lit room, sensing something very unusual was going on.

"Have a seat," Adams told me.

I sat in a swivel chair that was still in its shipping plastic. I found the chair comfortable and used my feet to spin around in circles.

"Jim, this is Jon Gruber," Adams said. I looked around, still spinning. The room was empty except for Adams and me.

"Who are you talking to?" I asked, stopping my spins.

Adams didn't respond. He continued speaking, it seemed, to the room in general. "Jon will be doing a lot of handyman work, but if you need help with simple things, you can ask him."

"Am I missing something?" I asked.

Adams waited patiently through the silence.

Then a quiet voice asked, "What if I blow a circuit switch?" The voice spoke with honesty and calmness like that of a child, and it filled the room.

"That I'll need to fix for now. In time, I'm sure Jon can handle things like that as well."

"Cool. Are you talking with a computer?" I asked, standing up from the chair.

"Yes," Adams said. "Jon, meet Jim. And he prefers not to be called a computer."

"Sorry, Jim." I looked around the room, wondering where to direct my voice. "Which way do I speak? Can you hear me okay?"

After a pause, Jim answered with a shy, "Yes." I noticed a green light on the wall over the largest desk. It glowed more brightly as Jim spoke.

I asked, "Is that your light, Jim?" He didn't answer, but the light pulsed gently.

Adams said, "It's an indicator of how much Jim is thinking."

It was my first conversation with a computer, and I felt a little awkward about what to say. Then Jim started asking me questions.

"Why are you here?" Jim began.

"I'm here to help."

"With what?"

"I don't know," I answered, letting my words trail off, still trying to grasp what was going on.

Jim's light stayed green for a while.

I looked around and made a mental list of what needed doing. I was happy to be offered more work, but I was especially excited to be talking with a computer.

"What do you think?" Adams asked me.

"When can I start?"

"Today I took on an assistant. I wanted to do this alone, but that was just me being stubborn. Familiar, eh Rose? A young man with a strong back and good hands. Mr. Gruber will do fine. Jim's taken a liking to him and vice versa."

- from p. 12 of Webster's journal.

The rest of this novel is available as ebook and paperback at major retailers and at Amazon.